Dare to
Dream

For foreign and subsidiary rights, contact the author.

Cover design by Sara Young

ISBN: 1 2 3 4 5 6 7 8 9 10

Printed in the United States of America

Dare to Dream

What if you were
made for more?

Dianne Weed

KUDU PUBLISHING

I would like to dedicate my book to all the prayer warriors that have prayed for me throughout my life—prayers that I often didn't even know I needed at the time.

Contents

Acknowledgment

Thank you to all my family and friends who have believed in me and supported my crazy ideas over the years. Thank you for being part of my journey.

Introduction

I know many people who are terrified of thunderstorms. Long before the thunder roars, they find themselves frozen in fear. I too may have found thunderstorms frightening if I hadn't had a father who loved them.

Growing up, we lived in an old home on the east side of Des Moines, Iowa. The attic was big with windows on each side of the peak. I don't remember there being a lot of things up in the attic except a double bed where we would lay during storms. My dad in the middle and my brother and I on each side. There we would wait with great anticipation for the next lightning strike to happen. All of a sudden, the attic would light up and my brother and I would quickly look wide-eyed at our dad for guidance. Soon we would all begin to laugh. I can still remember how the louder the boom, the louder my dad would laugh. He was teaching us that we have control of how we respond to things in life. Now, all these years later, thunderstorms still take me back to a happy time in my childhood and because of that, my focus looks different.

The words "Fear not" are in the Bible 365 times The same number as the number of days in a year. Isn't that interesting? God is reminding us that every day we are going to have to stand up to fear and not let it manipulate us. Satan knows that if he can get fear to control us, then we won't be able to live the life that God has planned for us.

Jeremiah 1:5a (NIV) says, "Before I formed you in the womb, I knew you." God designed each and every one of us on purpose, for a purpose. Knowing what that purpose is can give you the courage you need to face your fear and live the life you were designed to live.

I hope this book will help you find your purpose and then allow you to embrace the person God designed you to be.

Chapter 1

What if We Understood the Lessons of Our Lives?

Have you ever gone through something and wondered why God allowed it to happen? Life just doesn't seem to make sense sometimes and we find ourselves asking why. Why do bad things have to keep happening over and over again in our lives? Why does life have to be so hard? What if the reason is that we are a work in progress and everything in our lives, the good and the bad, is there to bring us into a relationship with God?

Before I was truly ready to trust Him with my life God had to take me through some really hard things. Things that would not just reveal my purpose in this life but also bring me to a place where I could trust God through the uncomfortable things in life. It's funny how we may believe in God and all His wisdom, but we often have a hard time believing that God could or would want to use us.

"Life is a succession of lessons which must be lived to be understood."
—RALPH WALDO EMERSON[1]

Socrates once said, "The only true wisdom is in knowing you know nothing." Were you ever in class and the teacher asked, "Does anyone have a question?" and all you can think is *I don't know enough to even ask a question*. That was me when God told me to start a non-profit that I would call The Twig, to serve children in foster care. There was no way I would have seen myself in this role. In my mind I not only lacked knowledge and experience, but I also didn't have time. How could I possibly do what God was asking me to do? Since that time, I have learned that it is okay not to know. God doesn't expect us to know. He just wants us to trust Him. God knows us more than we know ourselves. He knows what we are capable of and the things and people that we will need to help us do what He wants us to do. He has been slowly building our lives for this moment.

I have dreams for my children. They will often tell me that I believe in them more than I should, but the truth is I don't want them to limit their story because of the "I can't" in their head.

1 OSMQuote, https://www.osmquote.com/quote/ralph-waldo-emerson-quote-27eeff.

I know firsthand how easy that is to do. I want them to know that God believes in them. Why? Because it took me a long time to understand that - to understand that God would think I am capable of doing things I could never imagine myself doing.

Do you remember the movie, *Peter Pan*? At first as Wendy looked out the window she could only see so far but then she placed her hand in Peter's hand and went on a crazy adventure. This has been my Twig journey. Once I trusted God enough to take me wherever He wanted to take me I have been able to be a part of things that I could have never imagined.

As I began to share my passion for what I was trying to do during those early days at *The Twig* people started to come alongside me. Soon everywhere I looked I began to see God's provision. God doesn't send us out there to fail. Sometimes, we just need to look around us and deep inside to find it.

———

*"My God will supply all your needs
according to His riches in glory."*
—PHILIPPIANS 4:19 (KJV)

———

We may believe in God, yet for some reason we have a hard time believing that He would want to use us. Surely there's someone more qualified than me. Sometimes I feel like I am back in school standing in the gym surrounded by all the top athletes and suddenly the coach picks me. I'm not even really sure how the game is played and yet for some reason God wants me. Yep, life is full of "whys".

To fully understand how important we are to God we must take the time to look back to see Him in our journey. We must recognize the lessons that He has been trying to teach us throughout our lives and then for us to try to understand just why the lessons were there in the first place. Maybe we don't fully understand just how ready we are.

I remember as a kid thinking that once I was out of school I would never have to learn again. Oh, how naive I was. The truth is that our lives are made up of a succession of events that build upon themselves and create our own personal textbook for life. A book that is personally created for us to learn from. It is up to us to take the time to not just gaze upon it but ponder it and store the lessons we learn for now and for the days ahead.

When I was in the second grade, my teacher told the class that we would not leave second grade without knowing our multiplication tables. Well, I proved her wrong. To this day I still struggle with multiplication. Oh, I can get the answer, but since I do it my own way, getting to the correct answer is not easy. This seems to be the story of my life. My desire to do things my own way has often created obstacles on the path which God was trying to lead me.

Another lesson that God has been trying to teach me is about distractions. My mind has a tendency to wander all over the place, making it hard to maintain my focus. Many of our distractions may seem important to us but are they important to God?

When my girls were younger I remember telling my daughter to go clean her room. Hours later I went into her room thinking that surely she would be done, but in fact the room looked pretty close to how I had originally seen it. What had she been doing all of that time? Organizing her pencil drawer. She had gotten distracted, and that distraction kept her from doing what I wanted her to do. How many times do we get distracted from what God wants us to do?

Are the distractions in your life there to purposely avoid God's will or is avoiding God just a consequence of our distraction? Our lives are full of consequences that may not be obvious. If I decide to have oatmeal cookies for breakfast every day, I will gain weight. That may not be the intended consequence, but it will happen. Some unintended consequences can work out for good if we just allow ourselves to be open to what God is trying to show us.

I wasn't always the best student growing up. To be honest, I have always liked talking a whole lot more than I liked to learn. As you can imagine, that didn't always work out well for me. I suppose not much has changed in my life. To this day it can be my biggest barrier from learning what I need to learn.

My third-grade classroom had what was called a coat room. This room was basically a huge walk-in closet where we could store our coats, boots, and lunchboxes. That year I remember being sent to this coat room numerous times when I wasn't paying attention and talking in class while my teacher was trying to teach. Truthfully I was probably being more than a bit disruptive.

It wasn't that I was a bad kid, I just hated feeling stupid so instead of admitting I didn't know the topic that was being discussed, I would purposely get sent to the coat room. I liked being sent there because it was a place where no one was going to laugh at my wrong answers or the blank look on my face. The coatroom had become my safe place.

Not wanting to feel stupid has always been one of my stumbling blocks in life. Satan loves to use our pride to keep us from putting ourselves into a vulnerable situation. A place where we don't know all the answers. Where we have to rely on a God that does. I have finally learned, all these years later, that it isn't until we admit that we don't know something that we are willing and able to learn.

I can still close my eyes and see that coat room. The room was lined with hooks except for the one wall that had a window overlooking the front of the school. There, in front of the window was a stool that provided my perfect place to sit to take it all in. I can remember sitting there on that stool over the course of that year looking out at a large elm tree. A tree that was eager to show me the beauty of the seasons. Throughout the year I watched the leaves dance as they floated to the ground. I watched the snow pile up on the branches and I can still remember the sound of the birds singing in the spring. That tree taught me that seasons will come and go in our lives and even though each one may look different, we will find unique beauty in each season if we just take the time to see it.

My teacher will never understand the gift she gave me by sending me to that coat room. It taught me to not just go through the motions of life but to slow down, look at what God is trying to show me, and take time out of my day to observe the world in a way I can't when I'm busy doing all the things that the world tells us we "should" be doing. To be still and take time to see that God's miracles are always there if we just take time to notice them. I shouldn't have misbehaved, but sometimes it's in the consequences of our actions that we hear God most clearly.

THE DANGER OF BUSY

If you ask someone how they are doing, nine times out of ten they will answer "busy." For many of us, this has become our new mantra. It's as if we somehow believe that our busyness will validate our existence, as if we must be important because we are busy, so we fill our days with "good" things. What we don't understand is that our busyness is forcing us to set parts of our lives aside–parts that we can never get back.

My baby came to us ten years after the child that we always assumed would be the baby of the family was born. I suddenly went from being a "young" mom to an "older" mom, and that brought some challenges. During the time between my third child and this new baby coming into our home, a lot had changed in the world. For example, back in the 80's, babies were supposed to be laid on their bellies when we put them to bed. Now in the 90's, that was no longer the case. As every year passed, I was reminded constantly how much time had gone by since I had last done this. Now, play dates weren't scheduled by a simple phone call; you were expected to send a message through Facebook and hope that someone saw it. Yes, a lot had changed since that last time we had a baby in our house.

When your youngest daughter is graduating from kindergarten the same year that your oldest daughter is graduating from college you begin to grasp how fleeting life can be.

I believe that each of us will come to a point in our lives where we begin to question the things we have devoted the moments of our lives to. Where we suddenly question where our busyness has brought us, and more importantly, what it has taken from us. We think that life will slow down but the truth is life will never slow down unless we purposely slow it down.

When my girls were young our days were basically made up of just grabbing a kid and running from one event to the next. Our calendar ruled our days and as our obligations grew, I found myself longing for a quieter life. I suppose individually we were probably not as busy as it felt but combining each family member's obligations all together told a much different story. Our calendar was full and suddenly I knew it was my job to take a moment to step back and reevaluate how we were spending our days. I had to see if our busy life was taking my family in the direction that God wanted us to go.

As I sat down with the calendar, I began to see, not just all the things that we were doing, but also what we weren't doing. I began to study the calendar looking for the overlaps, those times when we were all together as a family. I soon began to realize that, just as I suspected, those moments weren't happening or at least as often as I thought they should. For the first time I realized that we were no longer spending quality time together and I found myself overcome with sadness. Even though we were all doing "good" things, this is not how I had imagined my family life looking like. It had always been my desire that my children would see themselves as a part of an elite team - one handpicked by God. They would become a team that would work together and always be there for each other no matter where their lives would take them. I knew that I wanted a family that spent time together, time to ponder life individually and time to come together and talk about what we are learning. My time back in that coat room had taught me that although time alone to recharge is important, I also learned how important it was to be with others. Relationships matter, and building meaningful relationships takes time. It became clear that I was going to have to make some hard decisions if our family was going to reflect those values.

We live in a world where individualism is celebrated and encouraged. Each one of us is doing what is important to us without taking into consideration how those choices could affect others. In our quest to find ourselves, we can unknowingly cast away our need for other people - people that are not just there to help pick us up when we fall - but people who need us too.

Ecclesiastes 4:9 (NIV) says. "Two are better than one, because they have a good return for their labor. If either of them falls down, one can help the other up. But pity anyone who falls and has no one to help them up."

We are stronger together but only if we spend time together. Football players can work individually on becoming the best football players that they can be, but it does them no good if they don't spend time with their teammates. This is what was happening to my family. Our priorities had shifted and I hadn't even realized it.

I now look back at that busy calendar and wonder if that is how God sees my life today, full of good things but yet no time for Him. It can be so easy for us to get caught up in the American dream, to begin to think that having bigger and better things in our lives will somehow fix the emptiness that we feel deep inside.

Hurricane Ian wasn't supposed to hit my hometown, and yet it did. Isn't that the way life is? We all know that there will be storms in life, but we never really expect for them to hit us. It's as if we believe that we are immune from ever experiencing tough stuff. Then one day there it is, coming right at us. Hours after the storm passed, I decided to take a walk. The farther I walked the more damage I could see. As I looked around at the devastation that the hurricane brought, I found myself seeing everything in a different light. Just a week ago there were people all around town that were making choices in their lives to impress others. They were spending their days gathering possessions that would make themselves seem more important. Today those same people are just like everyone else desiring their most basic needs. The storms of life do not discriminate but they do help us realize that it is not our stuff that defines us. Who we really are is who we are when we have been stripped of everything.

Who we really are is who we are when we have been stripped of everything.

When I was in the eighth grade my English teacher gave us an assignment that I have never forgotten. He wanted us to write what we would want people to say about us if we were to die thirty years from now. I wish I still had a copy of what I wrote. All I remember is that I said something about what a good person I was and that I was happily married with lots of kids.

Even though I was no longer hiding out in coat closets to mask my insecurities, I still could not imagine doing anything with my life that anyone else would notice. My plan was to do great things by raising great kids. Yes, living vicariously through my children started years before they ever showed up. This is a battle that I still have to fight today–to understand that God values my life too, not just the ones that I raised.

The next day my teacher had us write what we thought others would say about us if we died today. The moment that those words came out of his mouth my mind went blank. I had no idea what people would say about me, and I have no memory of what I wrote. The purpose of the assignment was for us to understand that we can't reach our destination without moving toward the goal. If we will take the time to look, we will find that we all have dreams buried deep down inside us. If we learn how to give those dreams wings we will have the ability to touch someone else in ways we never could before. Who knows, maybe someday they will be able to help someone else, creating a chain reaction and our little dream will suddenly be much bigger than we ever imagined.

"Therefore, my beloved brethren be ye steadfast, immovable, always abounding in the work of the Lord, forasmuch as ye know that your labor is not in vain in the Lord."
—1 Corinthians 15:58 (KJV)

LESSONS FROM MRS. NOAH

One of my all-time favorite people in the Bible is Mrs. Noah. She is a person who most people don't notice in the Bible but over the years she has taught me so much. Imagine Mrs. Noah going about her life when her husband just walks in one day and says, "God told me to build a boat." Now we aren't talking about just any boat, this boat was HUGE! We are talking five times as long as the Mayflower.

God told Noah His plans in detail but what about his wife? Not once does the Bible say that an angel came to Mrs. Noah to assure her that her husband wasn't crazy. Not once did she see the writing on the wall that explained the things that Noah was telling her. There was nothing for Mrs. Noah other than her husband's proclamation that all this was supposed to happen.

I wonder what Mrs. Noah was thinking at that moment. Did she just stand there with her mouth hanging open or was she so busy washing dishes that she really wasn't listening? Come on, you know we all do it. Someone is talking and we are kind of listening but not really. Maybe she hears the word "ark" and suddenly she thinks to herself . . . _what in the world is he talking about?_

Or maybe she heard him, but she just rolled her eyes thinking it was just another one of those crazy ideas her husband gets. Or maybe this time was different, maybe there was something about Noah this time that told her to listen up. Something that made her believe that what he was saying truly was from God.

Mrs. Noah has intrigued me since I was a young bride. I would love to meet her in heaven. I don't know if that is a thing but if it is possible, you will find me trying to track her down. I have so many questions for her. Did she grow to hate the view of that boat from her window? Did it cast an unwanted shade in her garden that frustrated her? Maybe Noah even cut down some of her favorite trees to build the boat. If so, I wonder how she felt about all that? I tend to be a rather opinionated woman so I am not sure I would handle it all as well as she did.

I can imagine Noah coming in after a hard day of building and being too tired to really care about her day. Did it make her angry? Did she hear the neighbors whispering behind her back about her crazy husband? Was she jealous of all the time he was spending on that boat? Did she ever doubt her husband? Did she wish that God had spoken to her too?

Don't you hate it when everyone else seems to know what they are supposed to be doing with their life but you find yourself just standing there asking, "What about me, God? What am I supposed to do?" I have found that God sometimes puts us on pause because He has things for us to learn in the pause.

Sometimes the pause is because right now he wants you to walk along with someone else just like Mrs. Noah did – to be a part of their supporting cast. He wants you to be there to encourage them or to help lighten their load. Having the job of supporting cast isn't always easy, but it is important. Noah knew what God had told him to do. His mission was clear to him, but did Mrs. Noah ever wonder why she was there? Did she wonder if her life mattered? Even though this woman had an incredible story, she lived with that boat in her backyard for seventy-five years and she didn't even get her name in the Bible.

The world will not always celebrate what we do. In fact, at times, it may seem to us that no one even notices us at all. I wonder if Mrs. Noah felt this way at times. Did she feel that what she was doing at the time wasn't very important at all? Maybe, but if I see her in heaven, I will be sure to tell her that she was an inspiration to me. She got on the boat!

We can learn a lot from Mrs. Noah yet there was no notoriety in what she did. She just did what she could to help Noah do what he was called to do. Mrs. Noah has taught me to trust your spouse when God speaks to them, even when you hear nothing. Like I said, she has intrigued me for years, but it wasn't until many years later that I came to understand why she would be so important in my life.

When my husband and I were engaged we spent hours talking about the perfect number of children that would be in our family. I wanted to be a mom for as long as I can remember. To us a huge part of marriage was building a family, but early in our marriage we were told that we would never be able to have children. These are hard words for any young couple to hear but we knew we were not about to give up on our dream of having a family.

Even though neither one of us had anyone in our families that had ever adopted, God was bringing into view for us just what our family would look like someday. I don't know about you but I don't change directions easily. Soon, however, I began to understand that we would love any child that God placed in our arms. It doesn't matter how they get there.

Adoption became a dream of ours, one that we didn't share with many people. The reality of why our dreams had changed was still raw. Letting go of a dream that you have is hard, but if we learn to be open to what God has in store for us, we may be surprised where He can take us. I know that I was!

Not long after our hearts were opened to adoption, we found ourselves busy raising three biological daughters. Yes, God likes to keep me guessing. I thought we were supposed to adopt but now I was beginning to wonder, *had I gotten it all wrong?* I couldn't help wondering why God had opened our hearts to adoption and then provided us with our girls. Yet as happy as we were, deep down we each knew that something was still missing from our lives. Eventually we shared our feelings with each other and decided that if a baby were to ever show up at our door, we would adopt that child. How do you like that for stepping out in faith without really moving? For years we thought we were being obedient with our willing hearts, but no baby ever came.

Have you ever found yourself thinking that you are willing to do whatever God wants you to do but for some reason you have never actually done it? Do you know that the Bible says "go" over 1,500 times? Over and over again He tells us to take action and yet for some reason we think He is just going to throw whatever we are supposed to do in our laps. Yes, the walls of Jericho came tumbling down but not until they began to march. The fish didn't just jump into the disciples' boats, they first had to cast their nets. God didn't shut the lions' mouths until Daniel was locked in the den.

———

"The definition of faith is your response to God's promises and command."
—MY DAD

———

It took years before we realized that a baby was not going to just show up at our door. We finally began to understand that God wanted us to stop talking about it and just move forward in faith. As I write these words, I realize how shallow they seem. The truth is stepping out in faith is hard. It is an outward expression–not just to God–but to the world. You are placing yourself in a position where others may question and challenge your decision. Stepping out in faith means you don't have the answers, but you know God does. As a couple, we were of one accord. Or so I thought.

For some reason I had always assumed that our adopted child would come to us from China. We hadn't talked about it, but I thought it was a reasonable assumption. At the time, China was a very popular place to adopt from, so I began to research just how to make that happen. In case you didn't know, I have found that God rarely does the obvious. He likes to stretch us and grow our faith in every situation that He can. Growing pains, whether they be physical or spiritual, hurt. Kids can't see themselves growing but they feel it and the same is true of our spiritual growth.

When I got married, the pastor recited Mark 10:8 (author paraphrase) "and the two shall become one". Chances are you have heard that same quote at a wedding or two. Now I admit I was young when I got married but somehow I actually thought that we would automatically, from that moment on, know what the other one was thinking. Wouldn't that make marriage so much easier? I'm not sure why but that isn't the way God decided to do things and it always catches me off guard. This was another one of those times. I told you that I wonder "Why?" a lot.

One day, out of the blue, my husband walked in and told me that he felt God wanted us to adopt our child out of the foster care system. Wait . . . What?! Where was this coming from? We had never talked about that as an option. There I was, just like Mrs. Noah, with my mouth hanging open. God hadn't told me anything about this change of events. Now to be totally honest, I had never really talked to God about what our adoption story would look like. I assumed I knew and then got busy making my own plans. This isn't the only time that I have been known to make a plan or two without first talking to God about it. Looking back, I now see that this seems to be a theme in my life.

I like to think that, just like me, Mrs. Noah stomped around the room and loudly explained to her husband why this wasn't a good idea, but in the long run she got in the boat, and deep down I knew I needed to also.

WHEN GOD HITS PAUSE

Yes, I was excited, but I also had a lot of fear and doubt. I was trusting that my husband–and God–knew what they were doing. We did not waste any time moving forward. We quickly took our parenting classes that the state required, had our home study done, and began decorating the baby's room in sweet anticipation of our new arrival. As we began to check each task off our list, our excitement kept growing and growing. Soon there was nothing more that we could do but wait. And wait and wait some more. The wait seemed to go on and on forever, with no end in sight.

Have you ever been in a place where it seemed that God had put your dreams on pause? The pauses of life are hard and those pauses can at times cause us to question what we once thought we knew. This was how I was feeling. Our arms were still empty, and we didn't understand why. There's that word "Why" again.

Soon my trust began to waver. Fear and doubt were building inside of me with each passing day. I have come to understand that all those times that I ask God, "Why?" I am telling God that I don't trust Him

I tried to bite my tongue to keep from saying, "I told you this was a bad idea." But I can assure you that my husband clearly knew I wasn't a happy camper. You see, I hate to wait, and he knows it. I had no doubt that we were supposed to be adopting but had my husband really gotten it right? Was our child really supposed to be coming by way of the foster care system?

I find in my life that the longer I wait for something to happen the more I begin to fear that maybe God has forgotten my prayers and because of that, I have a tendency to nag God and this time was no different. Over and over again I was telling God exactly what He should be doing and when. Do you ever find yourself nagging God? I am really good at it. It's as if He didn't really understand what I was trying to tell Him the first hundred times I mentioned it.

It has taken me a long time to learn that God will always answer our prayers but that doesn't mean that we will always get the answer we want. They sure didn't teach me that in Sunday School as a child - or maybe I only heard what I wanted to hear. The truth is that sometimes He says "yes," and sometimes He says "no," and sometimes He says "wait." The wait for me can often be the hardest. God doesn't give us signs like Disney World gives with wait times, so it can often be hard to figure out if it is a "no" from God or if we are just supposed to be patient.

Years ago, my daughter and I flew into Chicago for some one-on-one mother-daughter time. We jumped into the cab and told the driver to take us to our hotel. As we went up and down the back streets of Chicago fear began to grow inside of me. Soon every "Dateline" episode I had ever seen started flashing through my mind and I just knew that we were about to be taken to some abandoned place and chopped up into a million pieces never to be seen again. We were going to have to do something! Just as we were about to make our jump out of the moving car our hotel appeared right in front of us. Suddenly I realized that there was no need to fear. Our driver knew all along where he was going.

God knows the roads of our lives better than we do. We just need to trust the journey that He has placed us on. It's funny how I can understand that God is capable of doing so much more than I can ever imagine and yet somehow, I still have trouble trusting the way He goes about it.

During our adoption pause, God seemed silent to me. Months went by with no calls from anyone. I found myself wondering, "How could we have gotten all of this so wrong?" I began to wonder why He had sparked this desire in us if it wasn't going to happen. Do you ever start to second guess things when it doesn't all happen on your time schedule?

Trust the journey that He has placed you on.

It wasn't until a year and a half after we started our adoption process that we finally got a phone call from the agency. I can still tell you where I was standing the moment I got that call. I had come to wonder if this call would ever come, but here we were. The voice on the other end of the phone was saying, "We have a baby for you." I should have been thrilled. I mean, this is what we had been waiting for, but the truth is out of all the times that we could have gotten that phone call, this was not the moment I had imagined. I remember asking, "Now? Out of all the times it could have been, it had to be this weekend?" Once again, here I was questioning God's timing. You will find I do that a lot. You see we were busy, and as much as I wanted to say yes, I just couldn't see how this was going to work.

DO YOU TRUST BEYOND YOUR COMFORT?

I have learned that God loves to put me in situations that seem impossible to me. I hate to admit it, but I find that it is sometimes easier to trust Him when it is convenient for me. Do you find yourself trusting God only when His answer looks as you imagined? When His timing perfectly matches up to your calendar?

On this particular weekend I was in charge of a huge groundbreaking event that was taking place at my kids' school where my husband served on the Board of Directors. If that wasn't enough, we also had guests staying with us from out of town and my mother-in-law was in the hospital in intensive care following a terrible car accident.

Every one of those things involved people relying on me and I was already feeling stretched to my limit. To be honest with you, it would have been easy for me to tell them, "Sorry, this really isn't a good time." but I didn't. I couldn't. I knew that we had prayed for this baby and God was about to give us the desire of our heart. I knew I just had to trust His timing, even if it didn't make sense to me.

Looking back, I can now see that God always seems to ask the most of me when I am at my busiest. He likes to take me to places beyond my ability so I will learn to stop trusting myself, start trusting Him and realize that I will never be enough, but He always is.

Our baby girl came to us when she was just five months old. What I have come to understand is that God had a plan long before anyone else knew that a plan was even needed. At the same time we had started our adoption classes, her birth mother was getting pregnant. God knew that this baby was going to need a forever home. God hadn't forgotten about us; our daughter just hadn't needed us yet. We may not always see it, but God is always using the days of our lives to help prepare us for what lies ahead. God never wastes time; His timing is always perfect.

God is always preparing us for what lies ahead.

The older I get the more I can see the beautiful tapestry of my life and how He has weaved all of it together. As I write this, I am babysitting my granddaughters, my adopted daughter's baby girls. As I sit here, I can't help but get weepy knowing that because I stepped away from my busyness long enough to trust God, my blessings overflowed in ways I never could have imagined.

Believe me, I understand that God may be telling you to do something that might feel far out of your comfort zone, but do you trust God enough to be uncomfortable?

Has God placed *something* on your heart that your *busyness* has kept you from doing?

"The years teach us much that the days never knew."
–RALPH WALDO EMERSON[2]

2 "Ralph Waldo Emerson Quotes," BrainyQuote, https://www.brainyquote.com/quotes/ralph_waldo_emerson_100596.

Chapter 2

What if We Had Faith the Size of a Mustard Seed?

H ave you ever noticed that as kids start to become teen-
agers, they begin to think that they know everything?
I suppose we all did it. Life was simple back when we
knew all the answers. Unfortunately, the older we get the more
complicated life appears. Every question seems to have built-in
layers that we didn't always see when we were younger. Sometimes
those layers can make it harder and harder for us to figure out the
answers we are seeking.

The same is true with our faith. No matter how far we have
come there is more for us to learn. It's ok to tell God you don't
understand. To question and wonder. One of the greatest gifts

my father ever gave me was to learn to wonder about things. My mom had a strong faith, but she liked her faith in neat boxes. It made her uncomfortable to question God. My dad on the other hand saw the questions of life as faith-building moments. Over the years Dad and I would go for long walks and during those times I remember asking repeatedly "But why?" Dad would often have answers but other times the answer was just, "because that is how God made it." Dad was teaching me to rest in the fact that I may not always know the whys that life brings us but to learn to trust that God does.

———

"If you seek answers, you won't find them but if you seek God, the answer will find you."
—MARK BATTERSON, *THE CIRCLE MAKER*

———

I remember reading those words for the first time and they really resonated with me. My daughter had suggested that I read Mark Batterson's book *The Circle Maker*. She knew that I had been on a quest to find meaning in my life for quite a while. Have you ever been there? Watching your days go by and wondering if there is supposed to be more than there seems to be to this thing called life.

I had come to a point where I was grabbing for anything that would make me feel as if my life mattered. I desperately needed to see that I was here for a reason. I had walked through some really hard times, and I needed to know that God still had a plan for my life. I think most of us feel this way at some point in our lives. We want to know that our time on this earth will not go unnoticed, to believe that we have made a difference.

As I began to read one page of *The Circle Maker* after another I found I couldn't stop underlining passages. Suddenly I knew that God was speaking to me through this book. My eyes were being opened to things that I knew God wanted me to not just ponder but to experience in life. In doing so, I finally understood that I didn't need to ask God to show me the direction He wanted me to go. I just needed to seek Him and be willing to follow Him wherever that would take me.

Weeks after I read those words, I laid down on my bedroom floor with my face buried deep down in the carpet, arms stretched out in complete surrender asking God to use me *however* He saw fit.

For the first time in my life, I didn't need to understand what that would look like. I was just willing to trust Him. That moment changed everything. It didn't take long before God opened my eyes in ways I never saw coming. I was coming to God, for the first time in my life, with no agenda and no requests. When God opens our eyes we are suddenly able to see things that were always right in front of us but we had just never noticed.

In the seventeen years since we had adopted our baby girl, I had not once thought about her foster care journey or what her life could have looked like if we hadn't overcome our fears and stepped out in faith. Don't get me wrong, I was grateful for her foster mom, but the truth is I never really thought about the sleepless nights she must have spent rocking my daughter or all the other children that had gone in and out of her home. My daughter was mine and the road that brought her there didn't really matter to me. To me she was just as much my daughter as my other three were. I tell people that I threw her in the back of the minivan and never looked back. But all these years later, that was about to change.

It was suddenly my adopted daughter's senior year of high school. The years leading to this moment seemed to fly and suddenly the empty nest was fast approaching. I found myself wondering just how this next chapter of our lives was going to look. For thirty-six years I had dedicated myself to raising my children. I suppose some might be excited about this next chapter in life but for me it was saying goodbye to a life I loved. To a life that I was comfortable in.

Isn't it great to be in a place where you feel comfortable? To find comfort is a wonderful thing but we should not wallow there. Many of us, metaphorically speaking, have found ourselves in a huge comfy lounge chair that we just don't want to move from. That is exactly where I was. Yet like it or not my life was about to change, and I knew it. This was not my first rodeo.

By this time three of my children had already left home. In fact, my role as mother was now expanded to grandmother. You would think that since I had already seen one child after another leave home, I would have had an idea of what was to come, but this was different. This was my baby, the last child to leave my home. In my mind I was being retired from motherhood and I wasn't ready. Did you ever watch the show, *Little House on the Prairie*? If so, did you ever notice that as Laura got older, Ma was slowly written out of the story? I did, and I didn't want that to happen to me! Yes, I understood that my life wasn't really over just because my kids were growing up, but I was struggling to see myself in the next stage of life.

Life can bring us to a place that will cause us to question our past. We question if we used those years and our influence wisely, or if we spent too much time just going through the motions of life. These questions can cause us to question our future and what that future is supposed to look like.

I spent my childhood dreaming about my adult life. I was going to marry a tall, handsome man and have kids and live happily ever after. And I can tell you that I did just that, but I had never dreamed about what would happen once the kids left home. Suddenly here I was, and I found it a bit unsettling. I was very aware of the fact that my life was flying by. I could either see this moment as an end, or as an opportunity for a new beginning.

When change comes our way, we can choose to see that change through our own limited eyes, where we can miss so much. Or we can choose to try to see it through God's eyes–where a whole world of possibilities are just waiting for us to explore.

Our view is so limited if we only see the world with our own eyes.

Do you remember the first time you watched the movie *The Wizard of Oz*? When I was a kid, color TV was a new thing so when that movie started out as black and white it felt normal, because that is what we had always known. Then suddenly the movie turned to full color. I can't begin to tell you how amazing that moment was. Suddenly nothing seemed the same as it was before. I may have thought I knew what color Dorothy's dress was, but I really didn't. This is what it is like when we get a glimpse of how God sees things. Suddenly what has always been right in front of us looks so different.

As my daughter's senior year drew nearer, it seemed as if I was shopping all the time. We had senior pictures, dances, and award banquets. All of those events, in her mind, required new outfits. One day as I was sitting outside the dressing room, I began to wonder where my daughter would be shopping if she was still in foster care. I can tell you that in the seventeen years I had known my daughter, not once had I thought about the "what ifs" of her life. Yet now, I couldn't get the thought out of my mind. I began to think about all the kids still in foster care. If I wanted my daughter to shop somewhere that would treat her with love and dignity, wouldn't I want that for everyone else's child? I hate to admit it, but I found the thought uncomfortable. Why had I spent all these years not once thinking about all the other kids still in foster care?

When our eyes are opened to something that we feel we should have seen long ago, guilt can begin to creep in. Isn't it interesting how Satan loves to try to use our guilt and shame to bring us to a place where we will want to bury the thoughts that God is laying on our hearts? Satan knows that if he can do that, then he can get us to walk away as if our eyes have never been opened.

I couldn't do that, not this time. Only weeks had passed since I had laid face down on my bedroom floor to pray. There was no doubt that God had opened my eyes in that moment because He knew my heart was finally ready to receive it. As I set the guilt and shame aside that Satan was trying to throw at me, God began to place a dream in my heart that could have only come from Him.

I am good at seeing what needs to change in the world, but it is another to feel it in your heart. This time was different. Immediately I told my husband, "I know what we need to do!" As I began to tell him of all the things that God had put in my heart, I could feel the passion inside of me begin to grow. I can tell you that when your passion becomes a heart thing, you can't not do it. Soon big dreams were forming in my mind faster than I could say them. There was no doubt about it–these weren't my dreams. These were God's dreams. Lucky for me, my husband already knew the story of Mrs. Noah, and he had no doubt that it was now his time to get on the boat.

When your passion becomes a heart thing, you can't not do it.

GOD'S TIMING IS PERFECT

So why did it take me so long to see something that had been right in front of me for so many years? I don't know for sure. I do know that God had to place me on a faith journey before He brought me to this moment. A journey not to just open my eyes but a journey for me to learn to trust Him. A journey that took all the pains of my past and used them to grow a passion deep inside of me.

As unbelievable as it still seems to me, this 57-year-old grandma was about to become the Founder and Executive Director of a nonprofit called *The Twig*—a place where hearts could be encouraged, and God's love could be shown in a practical way. I could have never seen this coming. Even though I was surprised, God wasn't. I can now clearly see how He had been leading me here my whole life.

This desire inside of me wasn't just something I could talk about. God had placed a dream in my heart that could have only come from Him. I had to physically move in the direction He was leading me and boy was that scary. It was one thing to tell my husband but to tell others was a whole other thing. I remember the day I told one of my daughters what I was planning on doing. She is usually one of my biggest cheerleaders; but this time, instead of capturing the excitement I was feeling, she threw just about every doubt at me that you can imagine. I had been so confident, but was I wrong? No, there was no denying the passion inside of me. Her doubt actually made my convictions stronger. I remember pausing for a moment in doubt and then I looked at her and said "Yes, all that may be true but I just know God told me to do it so I have to do it." I remember telling her about how Jonah didn't listen to God, and he ended up in the belly of a whale and I didn't want to do the same. Looking back, I am surprised that my daughter's doubt didn't sway me, but deep down I knew that not doing it wasn't an option.

Telling those closest to me was tough so you can imagine how I felt when I first announced on Facebook that I was opening *The Twig*. I felt so vulnerable. What if I can't do this? What if people laugh at me? I can tell you that there was not one comfortable thing about opening *The Twig*. For some reason God had placed me somewhere that pointed out daily just how incapable I was for the job. Over and over I asked, "Who am I to be given such a task by God?"

I would love to tell you that I never doubted God, but that isn't really true. It's not that I didn't trust that He could make all this happen, but had He really thought out all the details? Not only was I, in my mind, not qualified for this job but I really didn't have time for it. I remember that one of my first thoughts was, good idea God, how about we do that next year? You see, not only was my baby graduating from high school, but my oldest daughter was getting married. Not to mention I had five grandchildren at the time coming in and out of my house on a regular basis. To me it seemed that God's timing was really bad. My calendar was booked but deep down I knew God wanted me to do this and I also knew that He wanted me to do it now. Just as God's timing was perfect when He had placed our adopted daughter into our arms, I needed to trust that His timing was perfect this time, too.

GOD ALWAYS HAS A PLAN

Three months after God first revealed the idea of *The Twig* to me, we opened our doors. *The Twig* is a place where children in foster care can shop for free each and every month that they are in care. Not only have we been able to provide positive, fun shopping experiences, but we have been given multiple opportunities to show them the love of God.

God took me out of my comfort zone and brought me to a place where I could clearly see His miracles on a daily basis. People love to say that God will not give you more than you can handle but that isn't true. The truth is that He loves to bring us to a place where we know just how incapable we are so we can fully understand just how capable He is.

So how does a college dropout/stay-at-home mom start a non-profit? The answer is simple: by coming to understand what God had been building my life for this moment in ways that I never saw. Some of my earliest memories are of being with my mom at the Salvation Army. My mom was the queen of thrifting and because of it, she could take the family budget and stretch it so much farther than most. The problem was that as I got older, I slowly started to become self-conscious of my mom's bargain finds. I started to notice that everyone else always seemed to have new clothes and I didn't. Soon I came to believe that I was the only one out there wearing someone else's unwanted things. I never said anything to my mom, but as a teenager, I remember being so afraid that my friends would see her car outside the Salvation Army and day after day my insecurities grew.

What I find so funny now is that I love hunting thrift shops for a bargain, but at the time it was just one more way that I felt different from everyone else. God had used those early years of insecurity to open my eyes today to how kids in foster care might be feeling. How "handouts" by well-meaning people might just be adding to those insecure feelings that they already have. The random puzzle pieces of my life were starting to come together. This is just one example of how I began to see the journey of my life and how it brought me to this moment.

As I started to design *The Twig*, I knew that I wanted to make a trendy boutique where kids in foster care would be excited to shop, a place where they would feel good about themselves and have a sense of belonging, and a place that would make them feel worthy of nice things. The problem was . . . how? How could I open a store with no money? I had a clear vision of how this was all going to look but I knew that it was going to take funds I didn't have. Our lives may seem at first glance, just a collection of random days but the same God that set the order of the universe in place has also set your days. Those days are much like a huge chess game with a plan to get us where He wants to use us.

Remember that adoption story where I learned that God often requires us to step out in faith? That lesson was important for this moment too. We signed the lease trusting that God would provide—and He did. Trust me, that was scary, but God continues to amaze me daily. When you allow yourself to follow God's dream for your life and walk a path you have never taken before you will find yourself at a place where you can clearly see God's workmanship.

My next hurdle was stocking the store. This place needed to be different from a "clothing closet" or even a nice thrift store. I wanted a place where everyone's eyes would light up the moment they walked in, a place where kids could feel good about themselves, and a place where they would feel loved and the parents would find peace. I wanted this place to be easy for the whole family to shop and I wanted everything to be free. If God has given you the dream then you can trust that He has a plan to make the dream happen. That doesn't mean that we are to just sit back and wait. Our job is always to do the best we can wherever God has placed us. When we do that He will open doors that we didn't even know existed.

I tend to see the world from the top down. This means that I always look at the best possible way something could be done and then I see how that can happen. God reminded me of my daughter's closet. You see, my daughter doesn't like to stand out in a crowd; so much so that in high school, she never wore bold colors or prints. Imagine my surprise when one day in the mall she saw a pair of red pants that she had to have. I questioned whether she would ever wear them, but she assured me that she would. Of course, she never did. All these months later, I began thinking about those red pants in her closet. If my daughter has clothes in her closet that she has never worn, then maybe other people do too. I began to ask around and soon piles and piles of beautiful clothes started showing up. Again, God was showing me that my past had brought me to this moment and I couldn't stop smiling. So many life lessons have come together for me on this journey and even though I couldn't see God working at the time, He was.

The first month *The Twig* opened, we served eight kids. I was thrilled. The truth is I didn't even know if we had any foster kids in our area when this all began. I was just doing what I knew God wanted me to do. We now provide thousands of shopping experiences every year to kids from all over southwest Florida.

Not only has it been exciting to know that He is using me, but it has been amazing to witness His miracles. I can't count the number of times that God provided just what we needed often even before we knew that we needed it. He is constantly reminding me that He is a good Father, our Provider. I remember the day someone donated size fourteen shoes. The shoes were so much bigger than anything we had ever had before. We all laughed and said maybe God has a big teen coming and we put them on the shelf in the back room. At the time we weren't seeing many teens, but that next shopping day Kevin walked through the doors. Kevin had to be about 6'4" and when I saw him, I started to grin from ear to ear. I quickly went up to him and asked him what size shoe he wore and he responded, "You won't have anything for me, I wear a size 14." I was giddy as I walked him back to the shoe department. I couldn't wait to show him how God had provided before Kevin even walked through our doors.

Repeatedly, I have been a witness to these miracles: the child that found her favorite outfit just like the one that she used to have at home, the brother and sister that hadn't seen each other for years and happened to come to the shop at the same time, and of course, I will never forget the boy in the wheelchair that could barely speak. He wanted a Tampa Bay Buccaneers football jersey. I was doubtful as I went in the back to look but there it was - a brand-new official team jersey. I thought he was going to jump out of his wheelchair when he saw it. These are moments that only God could have orchestrated. Once you begin to see the world as one big gift from God, you begin to notice how personal the gift is. When we take the time to look closely we begin to see that He cares about the details of our lives.

Through all of this, I have learned that if you want to really see God's dreams for your life, then you are going to have to be willing to do things that can only happen with God's help. We can step out in faith, but we have to continually trust God to do the rest.

"You don't have enough faith," Jesus told them. "I tell you the truth, if you had faith even as small as a mustard seed, you could say to this mountain, 'Move from here to there,' and it would move. Nothing would be impossible."
—MATTHEW 17:20 (NLT)

Take a moment to look back over your life. Look for the string that ties it all together. The lessons we have learned along the way are not just random lessons. Each one was taught for a reason. It doesn't matter your age, each one of us are continually adding layers to our lives that are working to grow us into our future selves.

Even though I had no idea where God was taking me over the years, it is now so easy for me to see how the journeys of my life have brought me here. It's okay if you don't know where God is taking you in your crazy life. He will reveal it to you in time, probably when you least expect it.

What have

your

life's
lessons

taught

you?

*"Don't bother to give
God instructions; Just
report for duty"*
—CORRIE TEN BOOM[3]

3 Corrie Ten Boom. *AZQuotes.com*, Win and Fly LTD, 2023. https,//www.azquotes.com/quote/392757

Chapter 3

What if We Set Our Fears Aside?

A few years ago, we hung a huge blank canvas above my daughter's couch in her new apartment. She had intended to paint a great piece of art to hang there but somehow, she had just never gotten around to it. We laughed and named the picture "Possibilities." I found that I loved looking up at that blank canvas. There was something about it that inspired me to think about what I might do with it if I just had the talent or opportunity to do it.

Many of us find ourselves looking at our lives the same way. Oh, the possibilities that life has to offer us. Yet sometimes we can find that blank canvas to be a bit intimidating. We find ourselves afraid we aren't good enough, allowing fear to prevent us from creating the life we once imagined.

"The world is but a canvas to our imagination."
—HENRY DAVID THOREAU[4]

I love this quote! If I could pass one thing on to you it would be not only to not be afraid to dream but to be brave enough to dream big. So many of us limit our dreams to what seems safe and allow fear to create the boundaries of our dreams. What if we didn't let fear stand in our way and we allowed ourselves to dream further than we can see—where the possibilities of our lives are only limited by our imagination? What would those dreams look like?

If you were to ask my eight-year-old grandson what he wants to be when he grows up, he would tell you: a spy, the President of the United States, and a gas station attendant. And he wants to do them all at the same time. Like me, this may make you chuckle, but when he talks about it, you hear neither doubt nor fear in him, just determination. It makes me wonder what each of us could accomplish if fear never stepped foot in our lives. Could you imagine what it would be like if you could once again live inside your eight-year-old head? What would it be like to dream without hearing the ever-present voices that tell us we aren't enough and that our dreams are foolish?

---

4 Henry David Thoreau Quotes. *BrainyQuote.com*. https://www.brainyquote.com/quotes/henry_david_thoreau_109604,

When a child tells you their dreams, you can physically see them light up with excitement as they imagine what it would be like. We may laugh but deep inside there is a part of us that wants to feel that excitement again and imagine the possibilities of our lives without the boundaries we have built. Somehow young children instinctively know that they are important and that they are here to do great things in life; but unfortunately, time will often squelch that, sending us to a place where dreams are nothing more than safe predictions of what the future will be.

———————

"May your choices reflect your hopes, not your fears."
—NELSON MANDELA[5]

———————

It makes me sad to think that my grandchildren may one day succumb to the negative voices in their heads. And it makes me angry that I allowed myself to listen to those voices for so many years. Oh, the years we waste trying to fit into a box that someone else has made for us and reside in a place where our dreams are silenced.

I'm not sure why, but over time we allow an ugly monster named "Fear" to come live inside of us. We begin to believe all the lies he tells us, like "you are not enough" and "someone else would be so much better than you." Before we know it, he begins to grow until he finally starts to take over our lives.

5 Lindsey Jacobson, "Remembering Nelson Mandela on the Anniversary of His Inauguration," ABC News, May 9, 2017, https://abcnews.go.com/International/remembering-nelson-mandela-anniversary-inauguration/story?id=47205398.

Most of us have lived with Fear for so long that ignoring him may seem impossible but if we acknowledge that he is there and that he has power over our lives, then we can actively work on moving him out. Until we do that our dreams will have no room to grow again.

Have you allowed Fear to smother your dreams? Have you buried them so deeply that over time you forgot that your dreams even existed? Take a moment and think back to your childhood dreams, back to when the sky was the limit. Can you remember how it felt to be invincible? When climbing tall things didn't frighten you or when you made something and you could see how wonderful it was instead of all its imperfections?

———

"The only thing we have to fear is fear itself."
—FRANKLIN ROOSEVELT[6]

———

SEEING YOURSELF THE WAY GOD SEES YOU

When I was in elementary school, I remember playing at my piano recital in front of the whole school. I had practiced for this moment, but when my fingers hit the keys, my mind went blank. Somehow, I had forgotten the song. I had nothing, but instead of panicking, I decided to just start playing random notes. Better than not playing anything at all, right? I was quite proud of my original piece of work and I was convinced that everyone else was enjoying what I was playing too.

———

6 Roosevelt, Franklin. 1933. "First Inaugural Address of Franklin D. Roosevelt." Transcript of speech delivered at Washington, D.C., March 4, 1933. https://avalon.law.yale.edu/20th_century/froos1.asp

At the end of my beautiful song, I proudly stood and took my bow. I remember looking over at my piano teacher with a big smile on my face, but then I noticed that she wasn't smiling. I suppose most of us can think back to moments in our lives that slowly took us from a confident child to an insecure adult. Fear has a way of slowly eroding our confidence and before we realize it, Fear has turned the possible into the impossible.

By the time I graduated from high school, I strongly doubted myself. I no longer thought of myself as amazing and my new mantra became "I can't." At this point, I was now very much aware of all my shortcomings and soon my days consisted of things I knew I could safely do without much chance of failure. I didn't realize it at the time, but Fear had taken over my life. The fear of being laughed at, the fear of making mistakes. I wasn't even twenty years old and the fear of failure was already stopping me in every direction I moved.

Soon I was at a place in my life where I wasn't even sure who I was anymore. As the years went by, I wore a lot of hats: mother, wife, daughter, and sister, to name just a few but who was I deep down? If all the things that I identified myself with were suddenly stripped from me and I was standing there by myself, who would I be? The things and people in our lives are a part of our story but they don't define us. Only we can do that.

I am blessed to have a sister who is fourteen years older than me, and I have found that if I take the time to listen, there is so much that I can learn from her. When I was in my fifties, she challenged me to think back to what I liked to do before I liked boys. I am not sure how this challenge came up, but I found myself caught off guard by it. Did such a time ever really exist? I began to reflect on the things that I had once loved to do and yet for one reason or another had not done in years. My sister was right. Around the same time that I started liking boys, I had begun to set myself aside in order to be accepted by others. I'm not saying boys were to blame. It is just a time in life when we naturally want people outside of our homes to accept us. We begin to think that if we dress and talk like the most popular kids, then maybe people will like us too. It's a great theory but if we aren't careful, we will soon find ourselves becoming just clones of those around us, with no remnant left of who God created us to be. We would walk alike, talk alike, and soon find ourselves thinking alike, leaving no room for what God might want to do through us. God made each of us unique for a reason.

If we refuse to see ourselves in the way God sees us, we will keep closing the doors He is opening. Doors that He wants us to walk through. The Bible tells us to love our neighbor as ourselves. The hidden message there is we need to learn to love ourselves. If you don't love and believe in yourself, your fears and insecurities will keep you from ever walking through those doors.

I don't enjoy being around negative people and yet at times I can find myself trapped with this person inside my head who keeps pointing out all my flaws. When I was young, I loved the mirror. I couldn't walk by one without catching a glance of how I looked. I am pretty sure selfies fill that same need for people as the mirror once did for me. It's a chance to say, "I'm rocking it!"

One insecure day after another changed that. Slowly I became more and more critical of the girl in the mirror until I just stopped looking at her. The person in my head had abused my self-esteem until I no longer liked myself at all. Do you understand what I am talking about?

The problem is when we no longer like ourselves, we will look desperately for others to like us. Seeking approval from the world will never be enough. Deep down, all any of us wants is to find a way to love ourselves unconditionally and to find acceptance in our own mind. One day, my daughter was looking for a dress for prom. We had been everywhere looking for the perfect dress and then we found it. She was glowing standing there in front of the mirror and I was so happy that she was happy. She went back into the dressing room to change and three minutes later she came out and told the sales lady she didn't want it. My jaw dropped in disbelief. "What happened?!" I asked. Come to find out, she had posted a picture of herself online and after two minutes she had not gotten a thumbs up or anything from any of her friends. Because of that, she went from feeling beautiful in the dress to feeling ugly. We had a talk and we bought the dress. She looked beautiful at her dance, but I knew that a bit of her confidence had been chiseled away that day. At first, I was so angry at her for letting others define how she saw herself and then I realized, wait! Aren't I guilty of doing the same thing? Learning to like ourselves is hard but until we do it we will never be able to love others the way that God wants us to love them.

When my fourth daughter was a baby, I took her to the Food Court at the mall. Not far from us sat a young mom with her baby. I watched this mom with a huge diaper bag and reflected back to earlier days, days when I too would bring enough with me wherever I went to help us survive anything that might come our way. I remember chuckling to myself as I looked at the one diaper stuffed in my purse. I thought I was in my own little world with my thoughts until suddenly this young mom ran over and started yelling at me. She began to accuse me of judging her for not having a nice stroller like mine. Then she disappeared before I could say anything. I still feel bad for any insecurities I may have placed on her. That was not my intent. To this day, when I feel judgment from a glance or a word I am reminded that my interpretation may be incorrect. It also reminds me to stop looking for approval from others.

Life has taught me that we all need to learn how to become our own best cheerleaders. There is only one person on this earth that is guaranteed to be with you throughout your life and that is you. Think about that for a moment. You are going to be with you your whole life so there is no one that has a bigger influence on you than the voice inside your head.

No one has a bigger influence on you than the voice inside your head.

We spend a lot of time in this life trying to make other people happy but how do we learn to balance that with learning to love who we are? I think it begins with truly grasping that you are God's masterpiece. God allowed everything that you are insecure about and the things you hate the most about yourself to exist. We may never understand why but we need to learn to accept them so we can learn to celebrate what is. So many years I spent looking at myself in a negative way and it is one of my biggest regrets. But it is also something that I have to make a conscious decision to not let seep back into my life.

Satan knows that if he can make us believe that we are just like everyone else then before long, we will come to believe that we bring no value to this world. I want you to hear me loud and clear: THAT IS NOT TRUE. It is a lie that Satan wants you to believe. We were made by an intentional God. You didn't just randomly happen. You were purposely designed by God, even those things that we see as flaws, God put there for a reason.

Wouldn't it be great if we could learn to embrace our true selves? To grab a hold of our uniqueness? To identify the emotional struggles in our lives and where those struggles have brought us? Every one of us has messy lives. God knows that. Embracing who you are doesn't mean that God isn't going to keep growing you. It simply means to set fear aside and try to see what God is teaching you. Let your life experiences shape you into the best version of you that you can be. Not a copy of someone else.

"You gain strength, courage and confidence by every experience in which you really stop to look fear in the face."
—ELEANOR ROOSEVELT[7]

---

7 Eleanor Roosevelt, *You Learn by Living: Eleven Keys for a More Fulfilling Life* (New York, NY: Olive Editions, 2016).

EMBRACE WHO YOU ARE

As I pondered my sister's challenge to recall my life before boys, it didn't take me long to remember how I used to love to climb things. Soon I began to think about how it felt to sit on top of the swing set or climb onto the roof of a garage and sit there pondering how big the world is. Up there I didn't feel small: I felt like I was a part of something huge.

When I was a kid, I climbed up to the very top of the inside of the Iowa Capitol dome with my dad. It is now considered too dangerous for people and is no longer allowed, but I did it. I can still remember the fear I felt as I slowly climbed those steps. I wondered if I would ever get to the top but when I finally did a sense of accomplishment came over me.

I remember the view being so incredible as I looked out over the city that day. It seemed as if I could see forever. Sure, I was afraid, but fear hadn't stopped me. I was only seven but at that moment I knew I could do hard things because my dad believed I could. I am not sure why or even when climbing became part of my past but for some reason it did. It would take me years and many struggles before I would look back at this moment. As I headed out to find a tree to climb, I remember feeling excited at the idea of climbing but as I got closer and closer to the tree, I could feel fear growing inside. The realization that it had been decades since I had done anything like this swept over me and the voices of doubt began to form in my mind. Standing there at the bottom of the tree, I looked up and began to wonder, "Where do I begin?"

Isn't it funny how we can complicate the simplest of things? I would describe myself as an overthinker extraordinaire. I can take the simplest of things and overcomplicate it so much that soon I find I am talking myself out of doing it altogether. Are you guilty of this? Yes, sometimes we need to pause but sometimes we have to stop thinking about it and just do it.

As I stood there looking up at the tree, I could feel the fear inside of me beginning to grow but I set aside the "what ifs" and just focused on the ultimate goal: to climb. So off I went. The higher and higher I climbed, the bigger my smile grew. I began to realize that I can still do hard things because I have a heavenly Father who believes in me. A Father who is cheering me on.

Climbing that tree reminded me of how much I have always loved seeing the world from a different angle - seeing things in a way that other people don't often see. At that moment I began to wonder if I was made for more than where my fear wanted me to stay. What would life look like if I was brave enough to dream a God-sized dream?

You were made for so much more than where your fear wants to keep you.

As far back as I can remember, I have always been good at seeing things in ways that other people just can't. I am like Charlie Brown and his Christmas tree. He could see that tree in a way that no one else could. The difference is Charlie Brown wasn't deterred by others' disbelief. He believed in his dream. As I paused at the top of that tree, I began to realize that God had made me like this for a reason. I am different from other people and that was okay. In fact, it wasn't just okay, it was intentional. I wasn't sure why I had been given this ability to see things differently, but as I looked around at the view from that tree that day, I had no doubt that there was a reason for it, and I wanted to discover why.

Stop hiding from who you were designed to be. Stop being ashamed of the fact that you aren't like someone else. Stop seeing yourself the way that the world sees you but instead learn to see yourself the way God sees you. We all need to learn to embrace how God made us to be.

When I was a kid, my mother used to say that she hoped I would have a child just like me someday. Now that may sound like a nice wish but it was always said when I knew I was driving my mother crazy, so I was pretty sure it wasn't meant in the most positive way. When my second daughter turned two, I knew without a doubt that my mother's wish had come true. This daughter was very strong-willed and I found it both frustrating and exhausting.

One day, when she was about eight, I found myself at my breaking point. Then, as I was about to yell at her for the hundredth time, I suddenly realized that God hadn't made her this way to punish me but to make her feel her convictions strongly. He had made her this way because He had big plans for her. Suddenly

I began to grasp that her strong will wasn't something I needed to break; it was something I needed to channel.

I remember sitting her down and telling her that God made her strong-willed for a reason and because of that she was going to be able to do great things for Him. I wasn't just saying these words to her: I truly believed it. At that moment I swear I saw a lightbulb go off above my daughter's head. I had turned what had been seen as a negative her whole life into a positive. I was giving her permission to be her. I am not saying that our strong wills never battled each other again, but I now saw her as the strong woman that she would become one day, one that would stand up for her faith even when others weren't.

You would think that having my eyes opened to how God perfectly made my daughter would compel me to embrace the way that God had made me, but that would take me a few more years to figure out.

Have you ever wondered why no two fingerprints are alike? I really don't think it is just so one day we would learn how to catch bad guys more effectively. I believe that God gave each of us our own unique print to remind us that each of us is on this earth to leave a mark that only we can leave. Our life matters to God. We aren't just one of the masses. We are each uniquely designed.

When I was a kid, my best friend and I dressed up just like each other. Now she was taller than me and we looked nothing alike, but we were convinced that if I squinted my eyes and if she opened hers wide that our mothers wouldn't be able to tell us apart. Of course we weren't fooling anyone but ourselves. As silly as that sounds, I now realize that I have been doing the same thing time after time in my life. Trying to fool the world that I am someone that I'm not. Stop trying to be someone else!

Has fear prevented you from living the life you were designed for? We can't change our past, but we can decide how that past is going to develop our tomorrows. What if you could spend the day back inside of your eight-year-old head? Back before you were very aware of your limits, back before you were trying to be like everyone else and fear ruled over your dreams? Where would your dreams take you?

I struggled with my identity for many years. I would hear of things other people have done and I could feel my sense of worth-lessness grow. I wanted my life to matter but who was I? Maybe you have had the same thoughts. I want you to hear me now . . . YOU MATTER! YOUR LIFE MATTERS!

When my kids were little, I taught them the letter M. At first, they just knew it was an M. Then they learned that the letter M had a sound. Later they learned that the sound was there for a reason and with that knowledge they could use it to write and read words. This is how life is. Some of us have never thought past the fact that we exist. Others of us may have realized our abilities but have never thought about the reason why we were given them. When we begin to see our abilities as unique gifts that are intended to be used to make the world a better place, then we will start to see dreams form.

There are some people who think they are just on this planet for their own pleasure and yet nature would teach us differently. Up until 1928, many people wondered why mold was even created. What purpose could there ever be for such a disgusting thing? I will admit that while cleaning my shower, I too may have had these thoughts once or twice; but the truth is, mold has a purpose. One day in 1928, Dr. Alexander Flemming came back from a holiday to find mold growing in his petri dish. He began to study the mold and soon he discovered it could kill bacteria. This is why we now have penicillin. This is a very short explanation of the history of mold; but the point is, if mold has purpose then don't you think that you do?

We are all here for a reason but for many of us, it may take a while before we are truly able to understand that. That's okay. It would take another dozen years following Dr. Fleming's discovery until it was used in hospitals - but look at all the people it has helped.

To really grasp that we matter in this world, we need to fully comprehend that we were made by God, on purpose, for a purpose. He doesn't make mistakes. He formed you in your mother's womb. You are His masterpiece. You are here for a reason. Until we understand that God has us on this planet for a reason, we will never fully accept our place in this world.

God has made us each a certain way and then has coupled that with our life experiences to allow our eyes to see things others may never see. Your story is for a reason. Someone told me recently that he never really understood grief until he felt it. Isn't that the truth? Each experience that we walk through in our lives will form us into who we will become. I wish I could go back to my younger self and tell her that it will all make sense one day. The steps and missteps that she made are all there for a reason. I would tell her to hang on to the person she knows she could be deep down.

Sometimes our life lessons will stretch us beyond what we think we are capable of enduring. We all find ourselves succumbing to doubt at one time or another in our lives, but it is faith that keeps us believing beyond the doubt. Faith can wash away our doubt if we just remember to run toward it in our times of trouble, grab onto it, and hang on tightly.

Instead, we have a tendency to focus on our doubts and fears. We allow them to control our lives. What if we set our fears and doubts aside? What if we learned to stop looking at what "is" and started to look at what "could be?" What if we could allow ourselves to have big dreams once again like we did when we were younger? What would your big dreams look like? There is a saying, "Love like you have never been hurt." What if you could dream like you have no fear? What would that look like for you? In a world where anything is possible, where does your mind go? What would you want to do if you were brave enough to do anything? What if we learned to take our eyes off of our fear and instead focused on the will of God?

"There are those who look at things the way they are, and ask why . . . I dream of things that never were, and ask why not?
—BERNARD SHAW[8]

I love how children from the same family can be so different. I have a grandson who loves sports. In fact, "ball" was his first word. Yet my other grandson, born just months later, would much rather be building something. How can two boys be so different? They were designed to be different because God has very different journeys for

---

8 "George Bernard Shaw Quotes," BrainyQuote, n.d., https://www.brainyquote.com/quotes/george_bernard_shaw_162023.

each of them. Each one of us has been formed at birth to be predisposed to have an interest in different things. When I was seven my best friend and I would spend hours playing that we were saving all the orphans in the world. I don't know why we started to play this but I can tell you that we both grew up to have an adopted child.

Our life experiences coupled with how God has made us allows us to see things others may never see. Your story is for a reason. You are here for a reason. Until we come to understand that, we will never fully accept our place in this world.

When my first grandchild came into this world, I was consumed with a love for him like I had never known. I loved this child instantly just because he is. He didn't have to do one thing to earn my love other than just be him. At that moment I finally understood God's love for me like never before. He loves me. He loves you. God loves us just the way we are. We all need to spend time trying to grasp that. Zephaniah 3:17 (NIV) says, "The Lord your God is with you; He is mighty to save. He will take great delight in you. He will quiet you with his love, He will rejoice over you with singing." God is singing over us! How comforting is that?! But it is even better than that, He takes great delight in us. Now I don't know about you, but I find that pretty awesome.

If God delights in us, then why do we work so hard trying to make everyone else in the world happy? We need to come to understand that love is not earned; love is freely given. We don't ever need to earn love from God or anyone else, we just need to spread love to a hurting world.

What fear must have gone through the hearts of His disciples as Jesus hung on the cross and breathed His last breath. Their guide, teacher, leader, and friend was gone. This is not how they imagined the ministry of Christ would go. Could they do this without Him? So much fear must have swept over them during those days but they took what they had learned and did what God wanted them to do. It wouldn't always be easy but with the help of the Holy Spirit, they found their way to spread the Good News throughout the earth and because they went on to reflect Christ's light, Christianity is now the largest religion in the world and it is all based on love.

Many of us will come to question life and our purpose at some point in our lives. We will begin to wonder why we exist and why we find ourselves in the situation that we are in. I wonder if those early followers of Christ wondered that too.

"You are not the darkness you endured. You are the light that refused to surrender."
—John Mark Green[9]

I believe that all of us have the same purpose that the twelve disciples had so many years ago: to reflect God's love to the world. Throughout our lives we will be given many missions, but that mission will always reflect our overall purpose. You might need to read that one more time. Your mission will always reflect your overall purpose. Missions will come and go in our lives. They will change us, but they will not define us. Never forget that it is

---

9 "A Quote by John Mark Green," Goodreads, n.d., https://www.goodreads.com/quotes/10036522-you-are-not-the-darkness-you-endured-you-are-the.

your purpose that defines you, not your mission. In other words, if you feel that God wants you to go help the starving children in Africa that is the mission that you have been given. Your mission is for but a season, but the mission reflects God and that is your purpose. Our purpose never changes. No matter how old you are or where God has placed you for this moment. Matthew 5:16 (NIV) says "In the same way, let your light shine before others, that they may see your good deeds and glorify your Father in heaven." Your purpose and my purpose is to reflect God's love to the world.

Did you ever sing that song, "This Little Light of Mine" as a child? In our house it was a childhood favorite. I love the part that says, "Won't let Satan blow it out, I'm going to let it shine." It reminds me that I have a choice. I need to not only protect my light, but I need to shine it in places that others will be able to see it. God has a plan for each of us and through that plan people will see Jesus. That is our overall purpose–to not hide our light or let Satan blow it out.

"Never let anyone—any person or any force—
dampen, dim or diminish your light."
—JOHN LEWIS[10]

Have you ever been in complete darkness? I have and I can tell you that the first thing you do is freeze out of fear of moving. In moments like those, it is easy to allow fear to paralyze us. We must always look for the light and move towards it and away from

10 John Lewis, *Across That Bridge* (Hachette Books, 2012).

fear. Throughout our lives God will send us many places. Each of us will have a different journey but all of us are called to shine the light of God, wherever we go. Your purpose is to let your light shine because someone may need to see it.

A few years ago, I traveled to South Carolina to experience a full solar eclipse. It was a beautiful sunny day as we sat on the edge of the lake. I thought I knew what to expect but like many things in life, there was no way of truly understanding until you have personally experienced it. There, in the middle of the day, the moon covered the sun, and the world went dark. I'm talking total darkness. I couldn't see my hand in front of my face, and I was suddenly too afraid to move. As I stood there perfectly still, I began to think about the day that Jesus died. Jesus said, "I am the light of the world. Whoever follows me will not walk in darkness. but will have the light of life" (John 8:12, ESV). Just as the moon reflects the sun, Jesus was here to reflect God's glory so we could not just see the light but feel its warmth. Yet as He died on that cross, the world suddenly went black. It is as if God was now handing the job over to the disciples to shine God's glory.

I remember sitting beside my father as he was preparing to take his last breath. I knew it was coming but there is nothing that can truly prepare you for that final breath. One moment he was here and the next he wasn't. I remember telling him right before he died that I would be okay and that I could carry on without him; but deep inside of me, I could feel doubt growing. Could I really? He had been my guide throughout my life. Loneliness began to creep in before he was even gone, but the moment it actually happened fear washed over me. I was suddenly so afraid. What if I was wrong? What if I really couldn't do this? I can't imagine what those disciples must have been thinking that day at the cross. How scared they must have been; yet, they did what they knew they were supposed to do, what they had to do.

———

"To trust God in the light is nothing but to trust Him in the dark, that is faith."
—C.H. SPURGEON[11]

———

LIVES INFLUENCE LIVES

We will never know the impact that we have on other people but God can take our simplest gestures and turn them into something amazing. When my grandfather was a teen, he went to a revival and gave his life to the Lord. This decision would not just change his life, but the lives of generations to come.

Even though Grandpa only had a sixth-grade education, he didn't let that stop him from pursuing what he felt was his calling. He went on to become an ordained minister and opened a little church on the east side of Des Moines. Providing for his family was hard as a preacher so, for a long time, he also worked in the foundry. During the week he would come home covered in soot from head to toe, then on Sundays he would dress up and preach, sharing with others how they could know Jesus. Grandpa did what he had to do to feed his growing family, but never lost sight of his God-given purpose. Oh, the hours he gave to provide for his family and serve his God. Not just prepping his sermons, but visiting the sick and

11 "Charles Spurgeon Quote," AZ Quotes, n.d., https://www.azquotes.com/quote/1411293.

taking care of the church building. He would not just mow his lawn, and the lawn at the church, but he would also mow the lawns of all the widow ladies that went to the church. I wish I could go back and ask him if he ever questioned if he was capable of doing what God had led him to do? Did he ever doubt himself or God?

Grandpa's church was never large, never more than a hundred people at a time, but he kept those doors open for over thirty years. As he was about to retire, Grandpa may have wondered at that time what his future held for him but he never lost sight of his purpose. For the rest of his life, he would continue to show the world Jesus no matter where God sent him.

You see, you never retire from God's work. I don't care how old you are, you are still here for a reason. Don't let the voices in your head tell you that you can't make a difference, or that there is no purpose to your life. It is one of the biggest lies that Satan will tell us; and unfortunately, we believe it way too often.

When Grandpa died, people lined up at his funeral to pay their respects to a man who had changed their lives. Grandpa had shown them God's love and it had made a difference in this world. We may never know the lives that we have touched. I am sure that Grandpa had no idea, but God knew. I recently came across Grandpa's life motto written in his Bible:

"I do not ask for mighty words to leave the crowd impressed.
But that my life may ring so true my neighbor may be blessed."

I love these words because they truly reflect who he was. Grandpa didn't just shine God's light from the pulpit. He shined it everywhere he went.

We don't have to do things that the world would see as grand in order to shine, we just need to reflect God's love right where He has placed us. We can sometimes think that obedience always means acting on something huge, but God can take our simplest gestures and grow it as far as He wants it to grow. My dad used to talk about how our lives are like the wake that a boat leaves behind. It may not seem like we are leaving an impact, but our life reaches far wider than we can see. There at his funeral I could now see that these people whose lives he had touched were the wake of his life. I was always proud of my Grandpa but at that moment, at his funeral, I felt that God was proud of him too.

On Grandpa's tombstone is the quote from Matthew 25:23 (NIV), "Well done, good and faithful servant!" I can't think of more fitting words to describe my Grandpa. A good servant doesn't question or argue, they just do what they are supposed to do and do it the best they can. That was my Grandpa. How did he go from an uneducated man to a respected minister? By learning to see himself the way God saw him instead of how the world saw him.

While we are so quick to see our imperfections, God doesn't see us that way at all. Yes, each of us will stumble and fall along the way, (even the disciples stumbled), but God isn't surprised by those stumbles and falls. Even though Satan would like nothing more than for us to give up, it is so important to remind ourselves daily that God is with us cheering us on.

SOMETHING TO PONDER . . .

What

would you

do if

fear

wasn't

stopping

you?

"Fear is a self-imposed prison that will keep you from becoming what God intends for you to be."
—RICK WARREN[12]

12 Rick Warren, *The Purpose Driven Life: What on Earth Am I Here For?* (Grand Rapids, MI: Zondervan, 2021).

Chapter 4

What if We Could Learn to Smile Through it All?

Growing up in Iowa, one of my favorite holidays was May Day. I can remember my mom and me gathering flowers from the garden each year and carefully arranging them in a basket that I had made. It was basically a cone made of construction paper with a handle attached. Nothing Pinterest-worthy today but I was always proud, nonetheless. After carefully arranging the flowers, I would take off on my bike and head to my friend's house, excited to surprise her with my masterpiece.

I remember approaching her house ever so quietly, so no one would know I was there, and placing the basket on the doorknob.

Then I would ring the doorbell and run off as fast as I could in hopes that she would never guess that the basket was from me.

The whole idea of a May Basket is to do an act of kindness in secret–no gushing about what a great job I had done making the basket or even receiving a thank you for thinking of her.

Isn't that a nice story? Wouldn't it be great if we could learn to be nice just for the sake of being nice? Unfortunately, most of us are more complicated than that. Oh yes, I made a basket for my best friend every year, that part is true. But when I got home, I fully expected a May Basket to be there waiting for me, and I can assure you, if there wasn't, my feelings would be terribly hurt. To me, that gift represented her love and acceptance of me. As if I didn't already know that from the long phone conversations that we had every day on top of spending hours together every moment we got.

I find that my expectations in this life disappoint me the most. Our days are full of them. We expect gifts even though we may say we don't want one. We also expect that traffic will have no hiccups, or that we will somehow have more time tomorrow than we do today. Every day, our expectation list is long. Oh, the disappointments we would save ourselves if we could truly learn to stop letting ourselves down with our expectations.

I also tend to expect to have time in the future to do all the things that I want to do someday but the reality is we do not have our hand on the clock of time. None of us know how many "some days" lay ahead of us and for that reason it is so critical that we take time to realize just how important each day is that we are given - it is a treasure that should be used wisely.

THE DANGER OF DISCONTENT

Years ago, we had one kid in college, one in high school, another in middle school, and one in preschool. Needless to say, our days were very busy. Each day was perfectly orchestrated, but it didn't take much to knock us off balance. We had stacked our days in a way that would work, only if it all worked perfectly; and of course, as you know, things never go perfectly. One particular day, out of the blue, we got a phone call informing us that my father-in-law had suffered a massive heart attack. Suddenly, without any warning, our world looked totally different and all the things that had consumed our minds only moments ago didn't seem to matter anymore. I remember as we sat in the hospital waiting room hanging on to each final moment with my father-in-law, my husband turned to me and said "Up until today, I have felt like I was juggling plates and doing a pretty good job of it. But now, suddenly, someone has just thrown in a piece of good china in the mix." What seemed so important just hours ago now seemed so trivial at that moment. We expected to have many more years with him, but our expectations were wrong.

We can spend so much of our life reaching for those things that are just out of our grasp that we forget how precious the things right in front of us are. Adam and Eve did the same thing. Have you ever thought about the fact that God had placed them in paradise and yet they weren't happy? Even in paradise they wanted more. Think about that for a moment. Out of all the things that God had provided for them, they wanted the one thing that He said no to. Adam and Eve were willing to risk it all for the one thing that was not theirs to have. The story of Adam and Eve shows us just how powerful discontent can be. Discontent can not only change our attitude, but it can also change our lives.

When I was a young woman, my father used to pray for me to be content. I hated this prayer. To me it meant abandoning my dreams. Couldn't Dad see that being discontent was going to improve my life in the long run? At least that is what I thought. The definition of contentment is "a state of happiness and satisfaction." My father knew that discontent can grow and if we aren't careful, it will allow us to justify a lot of things in our lives, similar to the belief that the grass is greener on the other side of the fence. Soon our eyes go from seeing what we have to lusting after all the things we don't have. Most of us get ourselves into trouble with one simple thought, "I deserve better." Soon we are willing to do whatever it takes to get what we "deserve." Oh, how simple life would be if we could learn just to focus on today. Not to expect anything from tomorrow, but to fully embrace the day we have been given - to somehow learn to dream big for today alone and do all we can with the day we are given, being thankful for the blessings He has entrusted us with.

When I was a kid, Dad told me that guilt is like a triangle that lives inside each of us. Every time we do something wrong the triangle turns, causing the points of the triangle to hurt us deep down inside. If we keep doing things that can cause the triangle to spin, we will find before long, the points will be so worn down that the triangle will spin freely. The older I get the more I understand this analogy. That twinge of guilt that we can feel deep inside is there for a reason. It's important that we do not allow our triangle to wear down. We need to stop justifying things with phrases like "just this once," "no one will ever know," or "I have no choice." All sin has consequences, even if we don't see it at first.

I remember a time in my life when I had completely justified something that I wanted to do. I had rationalized in my mind why this sin was okay: maybe it was not for everyone else, but it was for me. I was so convinced I was right that I shared my thoughts with a friend. My friend didn't try talking me out of it; he just looked at me and said, "So are you going to tell your dad?" My eyes got huge. Was he crazy? I knew there was no way my dad was going to see it the same way I did. My dad wouldn't buy my rationalization for one minute. At that moment I knew that God probably wasn't going to agree with me either. My justification had blinded me to the reality of my sin.

Justification can blind us to our sin.

The original sin had huge consequences that still affect us today. Adam and Eve did what they thought was right in their own eyes and because of it, God removed them from the Garden of Eden. He was going to make their lives a little bit less comfortable to remind them who their Provider really was. Ever since God has been using change in our own lives to remind all of us how much we need Him.

"You will never know that God is all you need until God is all you have."
—RICK WARREN

WE ARE A WORK IN PROGRESS

God will continually bring each of us to moments in our lives that remind us how much we need Him. God is the Creator of our lives. Until we fully understand who God is, we cannot fully understand who He wants us to become. Our lives have always been in His hands, taking us through things that will develop us into who He knows we are capable of becoming.

Have you ever heard of the works of Michelangelo called *Prisoners*? It is the sculptor's unfinished work that lines the way to the statue of David. I am told that it looks as if people are trapped inside the stones trying to get out. I can't imagine how moving this sculpture is. To me, it is such a parallel to our lives. God is slowly chiseling away things that are holding us back to help reveal who we are meant to be.

My cousin has started sculpting and I have learned that the first thing a sculptor does before he begins is dream about what the finished project will look like. To me, it may be just a hunk of marble; but the sculptor sees his dream for that particular piece of marble. Then as he begins to chisel away, he slowly reveals to the world what he always knew was there deep inside.

God has a dream for each of us. He knows what the finished project is supposed to look like even if we can't imagine it. God has dreams for all of us and if we pause long enough to look back at our lives, we will begin to see where He has slowly chiseled away things that were weighing us down. All of life's journeys have been designed by God to make us into the person God wants us to be.

Until we fully understand who God is, we cannot fully understand who He wants us to become.

I had a friend that got a job working construction. He immediately went out and bought himself a nice tool belt and some great tools to put in it. He was excited about the job ahead of him but as he began to admire himself in the mirror, he realized that even though he looked great, it was still obvious that he didn't know what he was doing. My friend had never done anything like this before. He began to wonder how he could be taken seriously when he knew it would be clear to everyone that he had no experience. So what did he do? He laid all his new shiny things out on the driveway and began to scuff them up. He smiled as he put the "used" tools back in the tool belt. He now felt ready for his first day of work. The problem was that without actual experience, the tools were still worthless to him because he didn't know how to use them.

Looking back over my life, I can now clearly see that God has been working on me for many years to grow my faith. He has not just been working to fill my toolbox with tools but to give me the skills to use those tools so I would be prepared when I needed them the most. Most of us can figure out how to walk the walk and talk the talk pretty quickly, but what about when we are faced with real struggles in our lives? Do we know which Bible verses to use to help us through those moments? Have our prayer muscles been built up strong enough that they flow off our tongues to keep us going when fear has paralyzed us? Is our foundation built on the rock?

God has walked me through quite a few hard times in my life. Times when I couldn't catch my breath. Yet as I look back, I can now see that each one of these experiences helped strengthen my relationship with God. Again and again, I would find myself back in His Word. I have learned that when we are walking through hard things, we can learn a lot from those that have gone before us. I grew up in a family where Bible stories were placed deep in my heart. The older I get the more I have come to understand that the people in those Bible stories had faults and fears just like we do and there is so much we can learn from them.

OVERCOMING REJECTION

Have you ever noticed that fear and anger are closely related to each other? Sometimes it can be hard to tell where one ends and the other begins. Many of us have been hurt in our lives by those that are supposed to care the most about us. There is no greater feeling of rejection that can come from their act of betrayal. This rejection can cause us to lash out in anger; however, deep down it is often fear that we are really dealing with. Fear that we will never feel loved again. Fear that we will never be able to trust anyone ever again.

There is so much we can learn from Joseph in the book of Genesis about pride, rejection, fear, forgiveness and so much more. These are emotions that we all will, at some level, have to experience some point in our lives.

Joseph was the youngest of his brothers and his father's favorite, which really irritated his brothers. (Just as a side note here . . . never have a favorite child. It doesn't end well). One day his father had Joseph go check on his brothers as they were tending to the sheep in the field. While he is there his brothers decide to throw him into a pit. His brothers not only threw him into a pit, they planned to do it ahead of time! For a brief moment, as they lunged for him, I can imagine that Joseph thought they were kidding but as he landed at the bottom of that pit, not only was he probably physically hurt but also emotionally. After a while, they threw him a rope and he climbed out, probably feeling a bit relieved, at least for a moment, until he figured out that they sold him as a slave to some passing travelers.

Can you imagine the feeling of rejection he must have been feeling at that moment? How lonely, afraid, and unloved he must have felt. Have you ever been blindsided by someone that was supposed to love you?

Rejection is one of the hardest emotions for us to get past in our lives. Rejection can cause us to begin to question everything in our lives. I am here to tell you that you can get through it and come out the other side with a stronger sense of who you are—Joseph shows us how.

Joseph had every reason to give up on life and feel like his life wasn't worth living. Instead, he rose to every occasion put in front of him over the passing years. Joseph didn't wait until his life was better to do the right thing. He just continued to do what was right no matter where life took him. That sounds easy but rejection leaves wounds and they will fester if we let them. It doesn't matter if he was in jail wrongly accused or standing beside the king in a position of power. Joseph just kept doing the next right thing. To me this means that somehow, Joseph allowed his wounds to heal. But how?

When I was a kid, I seemed to skin my knees a lot. Oh boy did that hurt, but soon the wounds would begin to scab over, and I would find myself picking at that scab until it would start to bleed again. I didn't mean to make it worse but I just couldn't leave it alone to allow it to heal. I find I do the same thing when I am hurt emotionally. I just won't let it heal.

Joseph had many trials ahead of him after his brothers sold him, but he kept his focus on the One that had always been there, even when he didn't understand what God was doing. Everywhere Joseph went, no matter how bad things looked, Joseph just continued to do the right thing. Joseph can teach us a lot about moving past rejection, but mostly he teaches us about forgiveness, complete forgiveness.

Fast forward many years later and Joseph has worked himself up from being a slave to one of the most powerful jobs in the land. It had not been an easy life for him, but he continued to do what he felt was right in God's eyes. One day his brothers came and asked for help from the government without realizing they were actually talking to their own brother. I think it is interesting that they didn't recognize him. Did his face show the scars of his life making him unrecognizable? Or was there a peace about this man that they never saw in the boy that Joseph was?

When they finally learned they were standing before their brother whom they sold, they weren't just shocked but filled with remorse. Joseph told them it wasn't them who sent him here, it was God. What they wanted for evil God had used for good. Joseph had every right to yell and scream and get revenge but instead Joseph's story was one of triumph and forgiveness.

When your life has been turned upside down, it doesn't matter whose fault it is. It is up to you to figure out how you are going to get through it and how your life is going to look on the other end. How we respond has the power to change, not only our character but our future as well - and it starts with who we blame for the situation that we have found ourselves in. Face it, we all love the blame game. It is as if blaming someone else will somehow make it all okay, but it won't. It is these moments in our lives that will define not just how we see the world, but how the world sees us.

I live in Florida and each summer, as a teen, we practically lived on the boat. As we would leave the dock, we would drive the boat at full throttle as we went through the inlet. Oh, the freedom we felt in that moment. The problem was that there was an elderly man that lived just past the dock and each time we went past his house he would come out yelling and shaking his fist at us. It wasn't that we were trying to upset him, we were just kids anxious to get to the ski bay. I am sure that this man has long since passed away, but I can't go past his house without thinking about him. I now understand that each time we drove by, the waves our boat created were causing damage to things that were important to him. Even though we didn't realize that at the time our actions were affecting him.

When someone else's actions rock our boat, it sometimes feels like all we can do is sit there and hang on for dear life. We often find ourselves frozen in time thinking they will come back and fix it, but they don't. Or sometimes we wait for that day when they will come to us and apologize, but we just find ourselves waiting and waiting. In those moments we must decide whether we are going to stay in the pit of despair or rise above it.

In the 1970s there was a psychologist named Harry Harlow who built a chamber that he called "the pit of despair". That is where we get that term. He would put monkeys in the chamber to see how they would react when he created trauma in their lives. He found that after a short time, the monkeys would stop moving around and just curl up in a corner. Does this sound familiar to you?

When our lives change, it is natural for us to want to jump in our bed and cover our heads. It is our self-preservation instinct kicking in. It is our deep-seated need to protect ourselves. Although we may feel that we need to do that for a short time to recharge, it is important that we don't stay there. Staying in the pit of despair will eventually destroy us.

We will be consistently affected by other people's actions. It's not a matter of "if" it will happen but "when." We can't change that, but we can choose how we are going to respond when it happens. Both the villains and heroes in the Marvel stories have a moment in their lives that defines how others will see them. We too will all have those moments in our lives - moments that could change who we are, for better or worse. It is up to us to decide how that change is going to look.

At a young age, I remember my mother explaining to me that being miserable only ruins your own life. Even though we may wish it would, it doesn't actually affect the person that has hurt us. She was right. That man on the shore may have spent the rest of his day stomping his feet in anger because of the wake of our boat, but we still skied and had a wonderful day. Being miserable for the rest of your life will not affect the one that hurt you. So, let's figure out how we can move forward.

First, we have to set aside our expectations. Stop waiting for them to come back and apologize. It may never happen. I never went back and apologized to the man on shore. I wish I could tell you that I had but my life had moved on from that moment until he was no longer there.

You may never forget what someone has done to hurt you but that doesn't mean that there isn't still room for forgiveness. God doesn't want us to focus on our past hurts or the people that have hurt us. God wants us to lay all that aside and just trust Him with the journey that is before us. That is what Jesus did. When Jesus hung on the cross, he said, "Father, forgive them, for they know not what they are doing" (Luke 23:34, NIV). The person who has hurt you may know that they have hurt you, but they will never be able to fully grasp the depth of that hurt. We all live with our own past pains, but we can never fully understand the depth of someone else's pain. The pain we experience is very personal because it is placed on top of the scars of our past pains, causing our pain to be uniquely ours - pain that no one else can truly identify with.

Anyone who has experienced rejection knows that it is one of the hardest emotions to get over. Rejection causes you to question your self-worth like no other experience in life. After experiencing rejection, it can be hard to learn to trust again–not just trust others or ourselves–but God. We must allow God to move us from the place where rejection brought us to the life He has imagined for us.

So, what do you do when someone has rocked your boat? What do you do when they never look back to say they are sorry? Matthew 5:44 (NIV) says, "But I tell you, love your enemies and pray for those who persecute you."

I know that right now you might feel like throwing this book across the room. Trust me, I have been there. I can tell you that during my darkest of days this was the last verse I wanted to read. Praying for someone who has turned your life upside down is hard, really hard, but isn't that what Jesus did? As He was hanging on that cross, people weren't asking for forgiveness. They were yelling, "Crucify him!" But he prayed for them anyway.

Praying for someone who has hurt you changes you. Trust me, I am speaking from experience. Now I am just going to go on and state the obvious here, these prayers are not for harm to come to the person that has caused you the pain you are feeling. Even though that may be what first comes to your mind Jesus prayed for forgiveness, and I think we should start there too. Ask God to help you forgive the person who has hurt you. Start praying for godly people to come alongside them. Pray that they would seek God's heart. When you pray for someone else's heart, it changes your heart in ways that you can't imagine.

RISE ABOVE THE MUCK

Not too long ago, I was walking in the woods, and in the middle of nowhere when I came across a bridge. As I stood there looking down at the muck under the bridge, I began to think about prayers and how they can raise us up above the muck that the world has to offer us. It's not that we won't still see what we were once wading through, but we will see it from a different angle.

When bad things happen, some of us will move quickly past blaming others and begin to blame ourselves. Self-blame may or may not be warranted; but regardless, it is not an easy thing to live with. In fact, if we are not careful it can destroy us from the inside out. Many of us can be quick to blame ourselves for every situation that life brings us. Deep down we may know that we have made some really dumb choices in our lives, but that blame can quickly bring us to a place of fear in moving forward in any direction because of the belief that doing so would only make things worse.

2 Timothy 1:7 (ESV) says, "For God gave us a spirit not of fear but of power and love and self-control." I want you to understand that every negative thought that you have about yourself is from Satan. Think about that for a moment. If we allow Satan to control the thoughts we have about ourselves then we are giving

him control over what those thoughts cause us to do and not do with our lives.

The other day I saw a mother on the news smiling even though she and her family were in the middle of great hardship. The news reporter was caught off guard and asked her why she was smiling. Her response really resonated with me. She said, "I must smile. It is important for my children to know that if we don't smile, despair will win." She is so right. We can't let despair win. If we allow despair to take over our lives, then Satan has us right where he wants us.

Has life ever brought you to a place where grief and fear has taken over your life? A place where you find yourself yelling, "Why God? Why me? Why my family? Why my loved one?" I have found that it is often moments like these that bring us to our first step toward healing. There is an old saying that says, "There are no atheists in foxholes." When our problems go beyond our ability to fix them, when we can no longer make sense of what is happening, we find ourselves running to a God whom we have ignored most of our lives or even denied existed. Let me tell you, God doesn't care how long it has been since you have talked to Him; He is just glad that you are talking to Him now. It is in these moments in our lives that we begin to understand that He has never left our side; and somehow, we have always known that deep down.

Like many girls, my daughters took ballet when they were young. They would spend their days spinning everywhere they went. How beautiful they would look for a moment but soon their world wouldn't stop spinning and no matter what they did they would begin to topple over. I remember their ballet teacher telling them that before they spin, they need to find something that could be their focal point. It was important that the item they picked was stationary so as they spun around and around, they would be able to quickly spot it. This would prevent them from feeling like the world was spinning out of control, allowing them to continue to spin with confidence.

When the world starts to spin out of control and everything you once knew to be true no longer is, you too will need a focal point. Hebrews 13:8 (ESV) says, "Jesus Christ is the same yesterday, today and forever." Someone told me recently that, "we need to learn to just glance at our problems and to gaze on Jesus." God knew we were going to need a focal point in life. One that would always be there when we needed it. Stop staring at your problems and instead gaze upon Jesus.

GAZE UPON JESUS

When I first saw my husband, I was in the seventh grade. He was holding a door open for a girl and from that moment on I was hooked. It would take a year of me following him all around school before I caught his eye, but the rest is history. We laugh because to this day it doesn't matter where we are or how many people are there, I can always spot him quickly. Why? Because over time I have learned the way he walks and the way he turns his head. If he is near, I just know it.

It is important that we don't just glance at Jesus. A glance is just a brief or hurried look. We need to take time to gaze upon Jesus. To gaze means to look steadily and intently. We need to look steadily and intently at Jesus and come to see him in our days. To know Him so well that we are able to spot Him in every situation of our lives. Proverbs 3:5-6 (NKJV) says "Trust in the Lord with all your heart and lean not unto your own understanding; In all your ways acknowledge Him, and He shall direct your paths." How can we trust someone we have stopped noticing?

All of us will experience times in our lives that frighten us. When changes in our lives come, it is important for us to understand that God has allowed each one of those things to happen. There is nothing in our lives that has not first passed through the hands of God. As I reflect back on the story of my life, I can now see the answers to so many of the "why's" that I asked over the years. Many things didn't make sense at the time but are now starting to come together to show me a God that has never left me—a God who has been there each step of the way.

One day during the summer before my seventh-grade year, I woke up and my parents said, "We are going to Florida. Get in the car." That day I said goodbye to my best friend, and without realizing it at that time, my life would never be the same. While we were in Florida my parents bought a house and left me with my sister, who already lived in Florida, for the summer. Mom and Dad then went back to Iowa and sold our home and my life changed forever. No longer would my grandparents live down the street. No longer would my best friend be there to share all my secrets with. From this moment on, everything would be different. I sometimes wonder what my life would look like if that summer had never happened. So many changes took place that year. Changes that would bring me to where I am today.

I have come to understand that we don't actually fear change, we fear loss. Loss of the life we know. So how do we make it less uncomfortable when we are going through loss? By figuring out what hasn't changed in our lives.

We are all going to go through changes in our life. We can't control that, but we can control our response to it. Being taken to a place where nothing was comfortable would cause me to question everything. Questions that, up to this moment, I didn't even know were questions. I found myself trying desperately to find my identity. How would I be known in this new town? No one here knew my family and my family knew none of my friends. For the first time I could be anyone I wanted to be. That is a lot of pressure for a twelve-year-old. I no longer wanted to believe in God just because my grandparents said I should or because my parents believed. Even though I didn't know it at the time, my move to Florida would give me a chance to grow my faith. I could finally make it mine and not just a faith that I inherited from my family.

Even though this time in my life was really difficult for me, I can now see it as an important journey that I needed to walk. After a few stumbles and missteps, I came to realize that my identity needed to be built on faith because without that, nothing else made sense to me.

Whatever you are going through right now, it is there for a reason. Learn from it. Evaluate who you want to be when you get to the other side of this rock in your path, and then move forward with confidence that God has a plan.

SOMETHING TO PONDER . . .

When

did your

faith

become

personal

for you?

*"The circumstances we ask God to change are often
the circumstances that God is using to change us."*
—MARK BATTERSON[13]

---

13 Mark Batterson, *Draw the Circle: The 40 Day Prayer Challenge* (Grand Rapids, MI: Zondervan, 2018).

Chapter 5

What if We Stopped Fighting for Control?

When I was a kid growing up in Iowa, I loved going to a place called The Ledges. It's a beautiful park where sandstone ledges tower over the Des Moines River. After a long day of picnicking and hiking, my family would never leave this place without first walking on the stones across the creek. A few years ago, my sister, brother, and I went back to The Ledges to relive our childhood memories and, of course, we all had to walk those stones once again.

As I began to step from one stone to another, I was reminded how much harder this was than it looked. Sure, some of those stones were easy but at times I found I really had to stretch myself to continue on my journey. As I proceeded, I couldn't help but think back over my life since the last time I had last done it. So many experiences have happened since then. Experiences that stretched me beyond what I thought I was capable of. As I approached the other side of the creek, I stopped for a moment to reflect on just how far I had come. The verse Psalms 121:3 (NIV) came to mind. "He will not let your foot slip. He who watches over you will not slumber."

As a very little girl I remember my dad leading me across this creek, always there to protect me along the way. Now, years later, I began to understand that it was a metaphor for my life. My heavenly Father has always been there to lead me one step at a time, even when fear urged me to quit. I may get weary, but He never does. Life is meant to stretch us. Every lesson I have ever learned has come from rising above what I thought, at the time, I was capable of.

I remember being so scared the day that I went off to camp. I was just a kid and I had never been in an environment where I didn't know anyone. The farther and farther we got from home the more I could feel my fear growing. My parents didn't send me off to camp to punish me. They wanted me to learn that I can do hard things and it worked. I learned that week that I could survive the uncomfortable in life and I need to remind myself of that from time to time. Every uncomfortable moment in our lives is not there to make us afraid but to help us learn something. Each one is a learning opportunity.

Throughout my life, God has put me in many situations that have made me uncomfortable. It has been in those uncomfortable moments, when I was stretched beyond my own capabilities, that I have reached out to God. These are the moments that would grow my faith in ways I couldn't predict - because it isn't in the comfortable that we learn; it is in the uncomfortable. When was the last time that you were uncomfortable?

It isn't in the comfortable that we learn; it is in the uncomfortable.

TRUSTING GOD WITH YOUR STORY

Have you ever read a book that you just couldn't figure out until the very end? I love a good book where the writer slowly adds in more and more characters and facts throughout the pages. It isn't until the last page that you finally can finally piece it all together and see what the writer was trying to show you all along. We need to learn how to trust God with our story.

Each step in our lives takes us closer to that moment where we can better understand that He has been writing all along in our upper story. An upper story is one that has always been visible to Him even though it may not have been to us. Very much like the front side of a tapestry compared to the back—we may not be able to comprehend how all the things we are going through will come together, but God does. As frustrating as that can feel at times, what if we could turn our frustration into fascination? Our frustration about things is most often from our inability to be able to control something, but fascination creates an excitement about what is and what might be next.

I remember my sister looking in the mirror one day at the wrinkles that were starting to develop and instead of being upset with them she looked at them with such fascination. How could something that wasn't there such a short time ago be there today? My sister has always allowed the world to fascinate her, even when it was affecting her.

How about you? Can you look at the ever-changing world and be fascinated about what might lay ahead instead of panicking about something that you have no control over?

———

"God, grant me the serenity to accept the things I cannot change, the courage to change the things I can, and the wisdom to know the difference."
—REINHOLD NIEBUHR[14]

———

The definition of serenity is "A state of being calm, peaceful and untroubled." I don't know about you but calm, peaceful, and untroubled are not how I would describe myself most days. There may be times when I can fool others into thinking I have it all together. I may

14 "Prayers for Serenity, Peace and Strength." Cincinnati Children's, n.d. https://www.cincinnatichildrens.org/service/p/pastoralcare/prayers#:~:text=God%20grant%20me%20the%20serenity,if%20I%20surrender%20to%20Your.

even be able to fool myself for a while but there is something about the middle of the night that reveals the truth. It is at this time when my peace can quickly turn into panic. Have you ever been there?

I find that handling stress can seem so much easier during the day but for some reason at 3 a.m. in the morning, my eyes will suddenly pop open and my mind will start to spin. At that moment, nothing good is going on in the world and I know that if I don't come up with a plan quickly, the world as we know it will come to an end. It's as if God has placed me in charge of worry and if I don't worry, the balance of His design will fall apart.

Now this may seem a bit overly dramatic to you, but it is honestly how I feel during those 3 a.m. wake-up calls. At first, I try to ignore it, but after much tossing and turning I just can't handle it anymore. It is at that moment that I have been known to run to my computer and begin writing emails to all the people that are at the root of this epic problem going on in my mind. Now mind you, it wasn't such a huge problem when I went to sleep but for some reason, now everyone needs my wisdom and they need it the moment they wake up, if not before.

As you are probably beginning to understand, I tend to worry a lot. I don't just worry about known changes in life, like kids moving away from home and planned changes such as "Should we downsize when they do?". I also worry about immediate changes. Immediate changes are those we don't always see coming until they hit us in the face. So how can I worry about something that I have no way of knowing is about to come down the track? Years of practice and training.

It's not so much "what is" that scares me, it's the "what ifs." In other words, change may come in ways that I don't want and quite frankly, that terrifies me. When we go through the door of change, we open up ourselves to the possibility of loss. Change is hard and it can often be scary.

I have always been a worrier. In fact, I come from a long line of people that suffer from this condition. My grandfather used to joke and say, "Don't tell me it doesn't pay to worry; half the things I worry about never happen." The truth is that no matter how much we want to, we don't have the ability to worry our problems away, yet for some reason we waste a whole lot of time trying.

Worry means allowing one's mind to dwell on difficulty or troubles. Allowing is the optimal word there. Worry is a choice. Let that sink in for a minute. When we are taking our focus and placing it on worry, we are choosing to do that. What if, instead of worrying, we could just be curious about what might happen? And what if we could learn to not let our curiosity turn into worry? I heard the other day that worry is us telling God that we don't trust him. I don't know about you but that really hit home. Do we really trust ourselves more than God?

"Worry is believing that God won't get it right."
—TODD WAGNER[15]

---

15 "Top 25 Quotes by Timothy Keller." AZ Quotes. https://www.azquotes.com/author/18107-Timothy_Keller#:~:text=Worry%20is%20not%20believing%20God,believing%20God%20got%20it%20wrong.&text=Legalistic%20remorse%20says%2C%20%22I%20broke,%22I%20broke%20God's%20heart.%22.

My husband once asked me why I keep giving it to God and then taking it back. At first I was taken aback by the question–but then I realized that (if I want to admit it or not) the truth is, I like being in control. I like to make a plan on how I think life should go and then, even if I don't verbalize it, I expect everyone to follow the plan. Wouldn't life be so much simpler if that was how things really worked? But life rarely goes as we plan.

Many of us like living in the fantasy of control. We like believing that we can steer not just our own boat, but everyone else's too. Our feeling of control is just an illusion that we have created. Somehow, we see ourselves as The Great Oz; but at some point, the curtain will be pulled back and the illusion will be exposed.

I have always known I am a control freak, but God had to bring me to a place for me to see just how bad it had gotten. I learned the hard way that God often uses change in our lives to teach us things that we are just not willing to learn any other way.

I liked my fantasy world called 'Control,' but one day, in a blink of an eye, it all changed. I didn't see it coming but suddenly my world completely spun upside down and I found myself beginning to question everything I ever thought I knew. We will all experience change at some point in our lives – divorce, job loss, illness, the list goes on and on. The change in our life may look different from someone else's change or even what we might have imagined as a possibility. It can catch us off guard and cause us to question the absolutes we have built our lives upon.

"Faith is not believing in my own unshakable belief. Faith is believing in an unshakable God when everything in me trembles and shakes."
—BETH MOORE[16]

I call this time in my life "my darkest of days" because during this time I never felt so abandoned by God. How could He let this happen? I felt so lost and alone. Not one person could truly understand what I was feeling. I found I was struggling not just with the grief I felt over losing the life that I loved, but also the fear that nothing in my life would ever be good again. I desperately wanted my life to go back to the way it was and yet the possibility of that seemed unfathomable. Not only could I not fix it, but I also couldn't figure out a way that God could fix it either. Trust me, I spent many sleepless nights trying to come up with a plan to present to God, but I had nothing. For the first time in my life, I had no hope.

Looking back, it's actually funny to me now. Well, not really funny–trust me, I still have trouble looking back over those days with a smile on my face–but it never really occurred to me that things were this way because God had a plan. To me it was more like God messed up and I needed to find a way to fix God's mess. Did that sentence hit home? This is the problem when we believe in God, but we don't really trust Him. Truthfully, we trust ourselves more than Him.

16 Beth Moore, *Praying God's Word* (B & H Books, 2018).

The other day I was talking to someone who is going through a time of deep heartache. He told me he was at such a loss that he didn't even know how to pray about it. At that moment I was glad that we were on the phone instead of sitting across from each other because I didn't want him to see the smile that was on my face. I tried to sound sympathetic but deep down I was excited. I knew that God was preparing him for a lesson on prayer. How did I know that? Because I have been there, and it changed my life.

Up until that moment I had always come to God with a well-thought-out plan–almost like a map–and if God would just cooperate with the map, my world would look like the way I wanted it to be. I wouldn't just tell God how I wanted Him to answer my prayers, I would give God very detailed plans as if He was a genie in a bottle and my wish was His command.

My prayer maps would look something like this: I would show God why it would be so important to get my daughter into a certain college. I would then go on and explain that, by doing so, it would allow her to meet the right guy so they could live a life that I had imagined God would want them to live. The problem was I never asked God if that was what He wanted for her. Why would I? The map worked if God would just follow it. You know that you are the epitome of a control freak when you want to control God.

During those dark days I spent most evenings lying awake searching my brain for a plan on how God could fix it. I wanted my life back the way it was, and I knew if I could just come up with a plan everything would be okay again. It's as if I thought that God had somehow fallen asleep at the wheel and it was my job to help Him get everything back on course. After days and days of searching for answers, it suddenly came to me. Now, as you read what I am about to share, you will probably laugh–but I want you to know I was completely serious. One day, I remembered watching a Superman show as a child. This particular episode was when Lois Lane died. She is the love of Superman's life, and he is heartbroken. He too was looking for a way to change the world back to how it was before. Superman comes up with the idea of flying around the world backward, thus causing the world to spin around in the opposite direction. This would allow the world to go back in time so that Superman could now save Lois from death. Yes! This was the answer I had been looking for! I knew without any doubt that God could do this. I remember how excited I was when I told God what He needed to do. I swear, in that moment, I heard God laugh.

I don't know about you but when I think of God, I often see Him sitting on His throne belting out a great big hearty laugh. I'm not sure why I see Him like this, but it might have something to do with being a parent. I remember years ago laughing the day my daughter came home from school and proudly proclaimed that 2+2=5. I wasn't laughing at her incorrect answer, I was laughing at her confidence. She didn't want to hear the truth. She was happy with her answer. That moment with God and me was like that. That day I was hearing God laugh and I knew it meant that I, too, might have the answer wrong. I remember how confused I was; what could possibly be wrong with my answer? How hard could it be for God to change the rotation of the earth? Faith wasn't the problem. I knew beyond a shadow of a doubt that God could do it, so what was the problem? It was at that moment that I came to fully understand that He was not just the God that could change the rotation of the earth, but He was the same God that had made the earth. And He did it without my help. Boy, was that an eye-opener.

"It makes no sense to seek your God-given strength until you trust His."
—MAX LUCADO[17]

Of course, I knew this on one level but somehow along the way I had forgotten that God was not my copilot. "Thou shall have no other gods before me" (Exodus 20:3-5, NKJV) came to mind. Had I placed myself above God? The truth is He didn't need me to come up with a plan, He already had one.

That was the day God burned my map. Have you ever seen paper burn? It is swift and when it is done it looks nothing at all like it did before. I now found myself with a new problem. If God doesn't need my map, then how do I pray?

Trusting God is a lot harder than it sounds. I had grown up in the church and every time I started to tell God that I trusted Him, another Bible story would come to my mind. I knew all those Bible stories well and I knew that they didn't always end pretty and that knowledge scared me. Was I really ready to trust Him, even if I didn't know the plan? Or worse, what if I didn't like the plan?

17 Max Lucado, *Life to the Full* (Nashville: Thomas Nelson, 2012).

Are you ready to trust God even if you don't know the plan?

The definition of trust is "the firm belief in the reliability, truth, ability, or strength of someone or something." I soon came to realize that up until this moment I had never really trusted God. Oh I thought I had but honestly my trust had always been in me. God had to bring me to a place where I knew I couldn't fix it to help me to fully understand that. It was in my helplessness I began to completely comprehend who I was speaking to. "I trust you, I Trust You, I TRUST YOU!" Those three words were all I prayed for days. I now understand that He was the only one I really could trust.

LET GO AND LET GOD

Have you ever watched a person try to train a horse to jump? It takes time. The horse doesn't naturally want to jump over the obstacles. They want to go around them; but little by little, the horse learns not to only trust the rider, but also themselves. It is a beautiful thing to watch once the horse learns trust. Sometimes, especially for those of us that hang on to control so tightly, God has to take us to a place where we can't see a way out. Sometimes it is only in our desperation that we will turn to Him–when we will finally come to understand that we just need to let go and let Him handle it.

During this time in my life, I was afraid that things would never get better. And even though I couldn't imagine how it could get worse, I couldn't help but wonder, *what if it did?* I had been trying to just breathe for months and now I wasn't sure I even wanted to do that anymore. Have you been there? Maybe you are there right now. If so, I hope the words I am about to share with you will help you as much as they did me.

On one of my darkest days a woman came up to me in the parking lot, looked me straight in the eye, and said, "Just do the right thing." It was such a random moment. This was a woman I hardly knew. How did she know the thoughts that were going through my head? Dark thoughts that were taking over my entire being and were not from God. I don't remember anything else that was said between us that day. Nothing else mattered. The moment she spoke those words I knew that those marching orders were straight from God.

That day I went home and started to apply those words to my life. Just get out of bed . . . it's the right thing to do. Just get dressed . . . it's the right thing to do. Just open your blinds so you can see God's blessings around you . . . it's the right thing to do.

At this time, I wasn't trying to focus on doing anything amazing with my life, I was just trying to survive, and it was working. My days weren't full of things I wanted to do but they were full of things I knew I should be doing. Day by day, I slowly began to break out of the despair that had held me captive. I began to grasp the idea that God had allowed my world to change, and if that was true, then there had to be a reason. I didn't know the reason and maybe I never would, but I was now sure God knew the reason. Before long I began to pray for God's will, not mine.

We will all experience times of change in our lives. Changes that will remind us that we ultimately have no control over our lives. Oh, we like to pretend we do, but the truth is the only control we really have is our response to the changes that take place around us. I am pretty sure this has been one of the hardest life lessons that I have had to learn thus far; the only control we really have in our lives is our response to the change we find ourselves in.

Each of us must come to understand that what we see as failure or devastating events, God can use as a teachable moment for us. He uses these moments to teach us how to rely on Him. Or maybe He is using us so others can see God in their own lives. Our only job is to do our best in the situations we find ourselves in, even if we don't understand why.

———

"Occasionally, weep deeply over the life you hoped would be. Grieve the losses. Then wash your face. Trust God. And embrace the life you have."
—JOHN PIPER[18]

———

18 Piper, John. 2017. "Embrace the Life God Has Given You."

We can't always choose the path that is put before us, but we can decide if it will be a story of despair or a story of thankfulness. My life has been a journey of ups and downs. I have stumbled and I have questioned. Yes, I can tell you that I too have screamed more than once "Why God?!" But if we are going to embrace the journey that God has ahead of us, we must learn to trust Him. Not just in the large things but in the small things too.

God places each of us on a journey to help us better understand not just ourselves but Him. To me there is no better example of that than the story of Moses. Moses was born to a Jewish woman at a time when the Pharaoh declared that all male Jewish babies were to be put to death. So many tears must have been shed across the land. Moses' mother couldn't bear the thought of her sweet baby boy dying. She knew she had to do something, even if it felt futile. I imagine that she must have made many baskets over the years but none so important as the one she was about to make for Moses. She took what she knew and did the best she could and released him down the Nile River. She let go of the situation and placed it in God's hands.

Isn't that a beautiful example of how we are supposed to handle situations? Take what you know, do the best you can, and then place it in God's hands and let go.

I would love to ask her what on earth she thought was going to happen to her son. I'm sure that she couldn't imagine that this was going to end well; but it would be just the beginning of the miracles that would surround Moses' life. I have a hard time letting go - doing all I can and then handing the situation over to God. If Moses' mother had not let go of that basket, then Moses would have never been raised in the palace. He was raised in a place where he would learn things, such as how to lead large groups of people. These are skills that Moses' mother could never imagine her son would need to know someday. God is a gentle teacher. He spent years preparing Moses for the mission He had planned for Him.

As a young woman, I took a spiritual gift test, and it said that I had the gift of administration. Have you ever taken one of those tests and thought they had gotten it all wrong? I did. In fact, I actually laughed at the results of my test. I didn't see myself this way at all. Sure, I have always been a strong-willed person, but is it possible that actually translated into a gift God could use? It would take years of God placing opportunities in my path to slowly teach me things that I would need as the Founder and Executive Director of *The Twig*.

Like Moses and me, God also has you on a journey towards something great. The journey started with the very personality that He formed in you upon your birth. It took eighty years before God told Moses to go out and lead His people–eighty years before he even began to understand what the lessons of his life had been about and he still had many more to learn. We like to rush our lessons, but God takes all the time He needs.

There have been many times in my life when God sent change my way. During those times I wish I had been given a burning bush like God gave Moses. Moses knew what God wanted him to do, but that still didn't mean that Moses agreed with God's plan. Surely there was someone else in all the land that was better equipped to lead the Jews out of captivity than he was.

Have you ever been there? Second-guessing God? He is clearly telling you to do something, but you are sure He has mistaken you for someone else. Many of us believe in God, but we often have a hard time believing that God could or would want to use us.

In the third chapter of Exodus, God is telling Moses His plan and Moses says, "Who am I?" In other words, Moses is telling God, I am not worthy of the task you want me to do. Have you ever said that to God? I have.

If God believes we can do it, then maybe we should just do it. Again, do we really believe that we know more than God? We tend to think that we just lack self-confidence but isn't it really a lack of faith in God?

God is never going to send us to a place where He isn't with us. God wants us to put our trust in Him and not ourselves. If we focus on how awesome God is, and all He is capable of, we should realize just how honored we are to be given a task from Him. Instead, we can't seem to set our doubt aside and neither could Moses.

Moses was eighty years old when God sent him off to rescue the Jews. I would imagine that he used his age more than once as an excuse as to why he should not be the one doing this job. I certainly thought I was at the age of winding down when God told me to start *The Twig*. We limit ourselves by the boxes that the world builds but God doesn't see us or the world that way.

I want you to take a moment right now and say this out loud: "God is so much more creative than me!" Now ponder those words for a bit. Do you believe it?

Think about the children of Israel standing at the edge of the Red Sea. I am sure they were surprised by the situation God had placed them in. They had followed His direction and yet here they were with the sea in front of them and their enemy coming up quickly behind them. There were probably a lot of "whys" being murmured through the crowd; I can't imagine what they were feeling by the time they got to the shore of the sea.

I am sure by this time they had lost all hope for the future they so desperately wanted. I would venture to say that not one of them probably ever imagined the Red Sea parting right before their eyes. God wasn't surprised that the Red Sea was there. He knew what was coming and He had a plan. That day they would learn that they had been placed right where God wanted them so they could experience God's power like they had never experienced it before. God had always provided for them and He wasn't going to stop now.

"Never be afraid to trust an unknown future to an all-knowing God."
—Corrie Ten Boom[19]

You too may not be able to imagine the situation that you are in right now ending well. Don't limit God to your own imagination. God used the Red Sea not to just rescue His people but to remind generations that His imagination is so much bigger than ours.

Like Moses' mother, it is important for us to do the best we can and then give the situation to the One who can do immeasurably more than we can imagine (See Ephesians 3:20). Our imagination is limited to what we know and what we have seen or heard. God's is not.

---

19 "Corrie Ten Boom Quotes," BrainyQuote. https://www.brainyquote.com/quotes/corrie_ten_boom_381184.

What

do you

need to

trust

God

with

today?

"Trust God for guidance in small increments; and if you can't see what lies dimly in the distance do what lies clearly at hand."
—THE RED SEA RULES

Chapter 6

What if We Learned to Overcome Our Busyness?

"Are we there yet?" I remember as a kid asking my parents that question a lot as we traveled. Each time my mother would encourage me to look out the window and try to enjoy the journey. I have come to understand that life is just one big journey; at times it will be wonderful and other times quite difficult. With all its twists and turns, this journey will define our relationship with God. Relationships take time and it is up to us to decide on what that relationship is going to look like.

Towards the end of 1958, my mother announced that she was pregnant with me–her third child. My grandmother looked at her in disbelief and said, "How could you bring a baby into the world at a time like this?" Her response has always fascinated me. You see, my grandmother was a strong woman of faith but instead of seeing my mom's pregnancy as a blessing, she viewed it as irresponsible. To my grandmother the world had become a dark and evil place. In her defense, she had lived through the Roaring Twenties, two world wars, a polio outbreak, the Great Depression, and at that time, the Cold War was just beginning. The story of my impending arrival has always reminded me that even the strongest believers can face doubts about the future. We are all susceptible to losing our focus. Our lives are so full of lessons learned and fears accumulated that it can become easy to focus on the fears rather than the lessons, but we must never forget that we are made for so much more than the fears inside of us.

Do you ever have a word that you hang up somewhere to inspire you? Try this word: PREVAILS. It means more powerful than opposing forces. Yes, you can overcome your fears because you are so much more than the fear inside of you.

You are so much more than the fear inside of you.

I had three babies in my 20s and I can tell you that there is nothing like having children to wipe away any small bit of confidence you may have once had. Just as you think you have figured it out, your child will move into a different stage or your next child will react totally differently to the stage that you had once thought you had mastered. I remember looking in the mirror and no longer recognizing the person looking back at me. When did my biggest dreams become a successful naptime? My life seemed unimportant and exhausting all at the same time. It is the first time in my life I remember thinking, "There has to be more to life." I now realize I was just caught up in the doubts and fears that this small sliver of my life had to offer. Now looking back, I can see that I wasn't just raising my children. While that is a very important job, I have come to understand that each trial and disappointment that came along in parenting, was developing me into who I would become.

God knows us better than anyone else does. He knows our strengths and our weaknesses. He knows the desires of our hearts and He also knows what will cause us to stumble. He is our ultimate Guidance Counselor and yet we often forget to seek His counsel. For some reason we think we can handle things on our own.

THE DISTRACTION OF OVERCOMMITMENT

Have you ever said yes to something and later wished you hadn't? Don't you hate that? Nothing can exhaust you more than being in a role that you were never supposed to be in in the first place. I remember one day when my children were young, someone called me to ask if I could head something up at the church. I was already feeling stretched to the max in life, but they wanted ME. To say I was flattered is an understatement and because of it I found myself tempted to say yes–not because I felt called by God to do it, and not that I even wanted to do it, but because I couldn't stop thinking about all the people they could have asked. But they asked me. My desire to say yes was simple pride. Pride can be a dangerous thing. I remember pausing for just a second before I answered, and I asked myself one question; "Do you truly believe that God wants you to do this or are you just saying yes because you were flattered they chose you?"

God isn't the only One who knows us well. Satan knows how to take hold of our ego and run with it. He loves to use our pride to keep us so busy that we won't even realize that we are leaving God behind. It didn't take me long to come to understand that Satan was trying to snare me deeper into his trap of busyness, and he was using my prideful spirit to do it.

Satan will also use our desire to please other people to catch us in his snare of busyness. As I said, Satan knows our weaknesses and he isn't afraid to use them, but God never intends for us to be so busy that we have no time for Him. It has taken me a lot of years to understand that just because I can say yes, it doesn't mean I should say yes. It is okay to say no to things in our lives that will distract us from God.

God never intends for us to be so busy that we have no time for Him.

In the Bible, there are two sisters named Mary and Martha. Jesus was a pretty big deal around town, and everyone was talking about Him and what He was doing. One day Mary and Martha's brother, Lazarus, brought Jesus over to their house. Mary knew right away just how precious this time with Jesus was and she wasn't about to waste a moment of it. She quickly sat at His feet, taking in everything He had to say.

Now, her sister Martha also probably would have liked to sit and listen, but she knew that someone had to get the food on the table. So, she was running all around trying to do what she thought she was supposed to be doing. In fact, she even told Jesus to ask Mary to help her. Then Jesus said, "Martha, Martha, you are worried and distracted by many things, but only one thing is necessary; for Mary has chosen the good part, which shall not be taken away from her." (Luke 10:41-42, NAS)

I don't know about you, but those words really hit me. I wonder how many times God has tried to tell me that I am keeping myself busy doing things that don't matter. Can you imagine how Martha must have felt at that moment? I would like to say that if I was Martha, I would have instantly understood and rushed over to sit beside Jesus; but the truth is, I can more easily imagine myself arguing with him, "What do you mean this doesn't matter? If I don't do it, who will?" I find that it can be so easy to get busy doing all the "good things" that we forget to spend time with our Lord.

It isn't in our busyness that we will find meaning to our lives; it is in our stillness.

It is important that we truly come to understand that it isn't in our busy calendar that we will find our purpose. It is in our moments sitting with the Lord.

WHERE IS YOUR FOCUS?

In the late 1600s, Susanna Wesley gave birth to nineteen children and home-schooled her children without the conveniences that we have come to expect. It must have been hard for her to find time to do all the things she needed to do in her day, let alone try to get some quiet time with God. Yet this creative woman did just that.

It is said that all her kids knew not to bother their mother when she sat in a chair and threw her apron over her head. As funny as that visual is to me, it wasn't to her kids, and it surely wasn't to Mrs. Wesley. This was her time with God. Isn't that just the best! Time with her God was a priority, one that she was going to find a way to make happen no matter how crazy her life was. I wish I could say that I am as disciplined as Mrs. Wesley. Her children went on to become great leaders of the faith. I believe it was not just because of the prayers that she spoke but because of the example she set. Mrs. Wesley's children learned at an early age that making time for God was important.

I admire this woman and her simple solution. I don't know about you, but I tend to overcomplicate things. I like to see myself as a detailed person - doesn't that sound so much better? Someone has to think about the details, right? The problem is those details can keep me from simply being with God. I have been known to head off to spend some time in my "prayer closet" and instead of praying I am thinking of ways to redecorate the space. Or I start praying for my family, which reminds me of their favorite food and before I know it I am making a grocery list. As I said before, Satan knows how to distract me. I have every intention to do the right things and then before I know it, I am getting distracted with the unimportant. It can be so easy to let the distractions of this world collide with our relationship with God. I don't know about you, but I can often get very distracted in life with all the "should do's" that I can have trouble seeing what I need to do.

Take Christmas for example. I have always loved Christmas. It's not just a wonderful time for friends and family but to me it is also a very holy holiday. Growing up, my parents were good about reminding me just what this holiday is really all about. Unfortunately, as I got older, I found myself not just trying to make Christmas perfect for my family, but I needed to make it more per-fect than the year before. How did I do that? By adding one more thing on top of one more thing to my Christmas to-do list. Soon Christmas was no longer "holy" for me, it was just "busy." I was preparing everything except my heart for Christmas Day. Does this sound familiar to you? Have you ever gotten to Christmas Day and realized that not once had you even taken the time to read of the miracle of Jesus' birth or thanked God for His Son?

One Christmas stands out in my mind more than the others. That year my days were full of activities that had become my Christmas focus. I was busy making matching Christmas dresses for my girls and making homemade gifts and cookies for friends and teachers. And, of course, in between all of that I was attending programs and parties and doing lots of shopping. Somehow over the years I had also come to believe that having a different-themed Christmas tree in every room helped the holiday spirit. When I look back at the pictures of myself during those years, all I see is one burned-out mama. I was trying so hard to do all the things. Things that I thought I was supposed to be doing and yet no matter how much I checked off the list there always seemed to be more to do. You see, I don't tend to compete with those around me. I am too busy trying to top myself - and that can be exhausting.

One day, amongst all the busyness, God spoke Psalms 46:10 (NIV) to me: "Be still and know that I am God." Deep down I knew that God wanted me to take time from my busy life to get to know Him and to understand His heart. He didn't care about all the things I was doing. He just wanted me to spend time with Him.

I remember looking around and realizing that not one of those things on my list was commanded by God for me to do. Not once in the Bible does it say that as a Christian our house must have the most Christmas lights in the neighborhood. Not once does it say we are required to rush all over to make sure that our kids get the latest and greatest thing out there to open on Christmas morning. I cannot begin to tell you how freeing that moment was. I slowly began to readjust my focus and move forward, and I have never regretted it. I now understand that I had become so busy throwing a birthday party that I had forgotten to invite the birthday boy. Can you relate? Christmas isn't the only time that we can find ourselves so busy doing things that we lose sight of the most important things. Jesus wants time with us, but not just on His birthday.

So how do we overcome our addiction to being busy? First, we must come to understand that, as with any other addiction, there is no cure.

It is something that we will struggle with our whole life. Satan knows it is one of our biggest weaknesses so it will be a battle that we will have to deal with daily until the end of our days.

I would like to tell you that ever since that Christmas, I have spent every day eagerly waiting to see what God wants to teach me, but that isn't true. It is kind of like my diet. Some days I am really good and other days I don't even realize how temptation has lured me. It can be so tempting to fill up our days and for some reason, for many of us, God can seem like the easiest thing to set aside.

Stepping away from being busy is something that I still struggle with every day. I have to consciously make time in my day for quiet moments with God. Some days it means throwing a grandkid in the stroller and taking a walk. Sometimes it means stopping at the end of a busy parking lot for a few minutes before I run into the store. But I do know that you can't have a relationship with someone that you don't spend time with so I am going to do what I can to find those moments.

SOMETHING TO PONDER . . .

Do you feel

closer to God

when you

are busy

or when

you are

still?

"Life is really simple but we insist on making it complicated."
—CONFUCIUS[20]

20 "Confucius Quotes." BrainyQuote.com. BrainyMedia Inc, 2023. https://www.brainyquote.com/quotes/confucius_104563

Chapter 7

What if We Looked for God in the Pauses of Our Lives?

I find that most of our life lessons come to us in the most unlikely of ways. A few years ago, I was sitting at church listening to the choir sing. Suddenly, I noticed a woman I had never seen before. I couldn't keep my eyes off her. There was a sense of calm and joy about her all poured into one. You could just see her love for Jesus all over her face.

She was well in her 80s and as I watched her sing, I began to wonder about her story. Could she really have gotten to this age without the pains of life being evident? How could she arrive at this age with such peace? I, too, wanted to rise above my story and walk into old age with a peace that passes all understanding (See Philippians 4:6), but how?

After church I hunted her down and introduced myself. Her name was Esther. Right there in the hallway I asked her to tell me her story and she didn't hesitate. She graciously proceeded to tell me all about her husband and how they had been missionaries. She smiled as she shared her story. You could tell that she had fond memories of the life she lived. Then a sadness came over her as she began to tell me about her son and how years ago, he had walked away from the Lord. I could tell that her son's decision still broke her heart, and then suddenly her face lit up again and she said with a twinkle in her eye, "He isn't walking with the Lord YET!" I couldn't help but smile at this woman's enthusiasm. At that moment I knew that she had no doubt that God was still going to do a miracle in her son's heart.

———

"The sovereignty of God is not a place where we will find answers to all of our questions. It is, however, a place to rest and trust that God is in control even if we do not understand why things have happened."
—JENNIFER MATTHEWSON SPEER[21]

———

The answer to this woman's prayers had been put on pause for years and yet she still had hope. I wanted to believe like her. I wanted to be okay with the pauses of my life. I wanted to be able to

---

21 Matthewson Speer, Jennifer, *Women of Grace* (Outcome Publishing, 2015).

smile knowing that God has a plan even if I can't see it. On that day, she taught me through example that our job is to believe that God can fix our concerns. It is our job to wait with great expectation for what He has planned. Instead, many of us can find ourselves prisoners of grief, depression, and hopelessness. Oh, how I want to be like Esther.

GREATER THINGS ARE YET TO COME

Today I was reading about Paul and Silas in the book of Acts. Here they were in the lowliest of places and what did they do? Sing. It doesn't tell us how long they sang but as they did the large prison doors suddenly opened. How did they feel at that moment? A prisoner is a person that feels confined or trapped by their situation. How did they feel when they fully understood that God was still in control? As grief begins to take control of our lives it can be hard to find a way out. Have the chains of disappointment bound you? Are you feeling trapped by the situation you are in? Maybe you need to just start singing. I did and it changed my life.

Not long after my map was burned, my sister-in-law asked me to attend a Woman of Faith conference with her. At the time I didn't really feel like going but I was trying to follow the "just do the right thing" way of life and I knew this probably fell in that category.

When we got there, I looked around at the crowd of women that filled the room. Everywhere I looked I saw women laughing and talking. I began to wonder if it was possible that I was the only one there with a broken heart.

Isn't it interesting how vulnerable you feel when you are going through something? Our pain can seem so obvious to us that we assume that everyone else can see it too. It's almost as if a huge spotlight is shining down on us for the whole world to see, making us feel very vulnerable. The truth is no one can really see the depth of your pain. Pain is a very private journey that can isolate us and, if we aren't careful, can cause us to feel very lonely at times. That is how I was feeling as the conference started. Here I was with thousands of women in the room and yet I was consumed with this deep sense of loneliness.

I kept wondering why I was here. How could I sit here and pretend I was full of joy when I found no joy at all in my life? The speaker's words were just background noise to my grief.

Then at some point they had everyone stand up and together we began to sing a song that I had sung many times before, "God of this City." Suddenly this moment was not about anyone else in the room - just me and God. He was using my feelings of loneliness to have some one-on-one time with me. Soon I found myself belting out these words, "You're the Light in this darkness. You're the Peace to the restless . . . Greater things are still to be done. . . ."

There, surrounded by thousands of women, God had a very personal message to me. "Greater things are yet to come." I couldn't stop singing those words over and over again. I knew that in this huge crowd of ladies God was personally giving me a vision of hope. He was letting me know that He had a plan for my life. I just needed to trust Him. It was as if He had opened my prison doors. Suddenly, I understood that I was right where God wanted me. He wanted me in a place where He could grow my faith in ways I couldn't imagine. He had brought me through my hardest days to open my eyes to His endless possibilities. I just needed to learn to trust Him. God was assuring me that there was a plan. Jeremiah 29:11 (NIV) says "'For I know that plans I have for you,' declares the Lord, 'plans to give you hope and a future.'" For once in my life, I was okay not knowing the plan. Just knowing that there was a plan brought comfort to my soul and gave me hope.

Do you feel trapped by grief? Has fear made you a prisoner? God doesn't just have a plan for *my* life. He has one for yours too.

Fear, pain, and loss can make us feel as if we are roaming around in a desert all alone. But the Bible tells us that God is our refuge and our fortress. He is our safe place. Imagine being out in the desert all alone and feeling lost and then suddenly you see this fortress right there. This is how I felt at that moment. Suddenly I knew I was in a safe place, in the arms of Jesus.

"Hope is that thing inside us that insists, despite all the evidence to the contrary, that something better awaits us if we have the courage to reach for it and to work for it and to fight for it."
—BARACK OBAMA[22]

PRAYING THROUGH THE PAUSES

I want you to understand that nothing significant changed in my life in the days that followed. I did not wake up the next day without a care in the world; but inside, everything was different. I now had confidence that I was going to get through these dark days. God had told me He had plans for me, and I was ready for

22 Obama, Barack. 2008. "Iowa Caucus Victory Speech." Transcript of speech delivered at Des Moines, January 3, 2008. https://www.nytimes.com/2008/01/03/us/politics/03obama-transcript.html.

them! Suddenly my life didn't seem so dark anymore because I could now see a glimmer of light.

Most of us want to leap right out of our prison walls and hit the ground running and I was no different. I was ready to do mighty things for the One who had given me hope but as the days and months passed, I found myself desperate for direction in my life. I was trying hard to not once again start writing those maps for God again, but I will admit the silence of the pause God had now placed me in was hard.

I was eager but for some reason God wasn't giving me my marching orders. God had changed my prayers in a dramatic way the day He burned my map, yet there was so much more for me to learn. God wanted me to see Him in a way that I never had before. To learn to trust Him more than I trust myself. The pause was hard, but I can tell you it was worth it.

I have since learned that the Bible is full of what I call "hidden waits." We tend to read right past them, but they are there. Times when things didn't happen in a flash or even overnight. The children of Israel didn't have to wander around the wilderness for forty years. God could have just beamed them there in a flash, but they had things they needed to learn along the way, and so do we. Or remember Joseph? He waited years before he was reunited with his family. We are not the first people that God has told, "Not yet." Reflect back over your own life and I am sure you will find many times that you have felt God has hit the pause button. Can you now understand why he had you wait?

I am a firm believer that you can't know where you are going if you don't know where you have been. God has placed all of us on a journey and many of us don't even know it. He has provided lessons for us to learn along the way and touch the lives of others. It is important that we take time to look back over our lives to see where our journey is leading us. We must cast our cares aside so we can move forward. Instead, we often find ourselves dragging our burdens with us. We wrap ourselves up in them and carry them with us throughout our lives almost as a badge of honor.

Who are you without the weight of your burdens that you have gathered along life's way? If you were to lay your insecurities down, who would you be? Who would you be if you were to allow yourself to dream again? There is so much we can learn from life's pauses, but it is up to us to take those lessons and apply them to our lives.

There are three important elements of our lives that we must not neglect: planning, doing, and reflecting. Each one of these things are equally as important as the other and not one of them should be neglected.

There are many people that are great planners and love doing great things but they can often neglect taking time to reflect on the experiences they have had. Luke 2:19 says that Mary, the mother of Jesus, pondered these things in her heart. Some translations say she stored these things in her heart. I think Mary knew that her life ahead was not going to be easy. God wanted her to store those things in her heart so she could come back to them when she would find herself doubting if she was strong enough, when she was feeling afraid, and when the voices in her head would start to make her feel unworthy of the journey God had placed her on.

Which of these do you need to work on most? Planning, doing, or reflecting? I will admit that it is often the first one that trips me up the most often. Oh, I love to plan but I can easily neglect taking the time to see if my plan lines up with God's plan. Instead I jump right into doing what I think I "should" be doing. God is working on this with me, but it is definitely my weakness. It may "feel" right to me so I don't spend time in prayer about it or I assume that other people have prayed about it; so if they are on board, I should be too.

Are you also guilty of delegating your prayers? It's okay to ask others to pray for a situation but we need to make sure that we, too, are praying. We have a direct line to the One who designed the universe and yet we often don't take the time to consult with Him. In many ways, we are just like a three-year-old, determined to do it ourselves.

"You can do more than pray after you pray. But you cannot do more than pray until you pray."
—My Grandpa

Some of us spend a whole lot of time talking to God about what we should do but we never actually make a move in the direction God has told us to go. Unfortunately we often end up getting too comfortable in the pauses of life instead. The pauses of our lives are there for us to learn from but it is vital that we don't stay in them longer than we are supposed to.

My grandsons are staying with me right now, and getting them out of the house can sometimes be a chore. It always seems there is one more thing they need to do before we can go. I wonder if we seem that way to God.

We can often find it easy to find reasons not to step out in faith. This is where faith steps in. We will not always know how things are going to turn out but if we feel deep down in our soul that we are supposed to do something, then we need to do it. David didn't overthink taking on Goliath. Those around him wanted to weigh him down with how they thought he should proceed but David just stepped out on that field. How vulnerable and maybe even a bit foolish he must have seemed to others, but he had unbelievable faith that he was doing what he was supposed to do. It is easy to think of people in the Bible as superheroes—but they weren't. They were just ordinary people that stepped out in faith.

Pauses in our lives are not just there for a reason, they are there for a certain amount of time. This is a time that we need to be in active prayer. These prayers are not so God can hear us, but so our hearts would be open to hearing Him. Prayer opens our eyes to see the blessings and opportunities all around us that will touch the life of someone else.

Sometimes when we are looking for large impactful things to do, we miss the small things that God has set before us. That woman who was singing in the choir was using her talents and her story. By doing so, she inspired me. Over and over, I can see times in my life when the right person has been there to teach me and encourage me to keep moving forward. I pray that God will use my faith to encourage someone else someday.

"Every step of faith not only moves us forward, but leaves a footprint behind for others coming after us to see."
—Written in my Grandpa's Bible

SEEING YOURSELF THROUGH GOD'S EYES

Some of us are good about doing what God tells us to do, but we don't take the time to reflect on it afterward. I call these "forward motion people." These people view pausing to reflect as a waste of time. I believe that our greatest lessons in this life will be discovered as we take time to reflect back–times when we pause and count our blessings.

My mother used to say that sometimes God puts us flat on our backs so all we can do is look up. She was so right. I started writing this book when I was isolated because of Covid. For years people have told me that I should write a book, but I never knew what that book should be about. It wasn't until I paused to look back over my life that I realized that I had a story–a story I could learn from–if I would just take the time.

God is in each chapter of our lives if we just take the time to look. We must grasp what He has brought us through before we can fully trust where He wants to take us next.

I find that when God hits the pause button on my life, it can be so tempting for me to start drawing those maps again. Isn't that the way we are? We know better but if we aren't careful, we go right back to where we started, as if we had forgotten all we have learned along the way.

In the first chapter of Acts, Jesus is hanging out with his disciples. Here they are talking with Jesus, who they had just seen killed a few days ago and whose body is no longer in the tomb. At this moment, the disciples were finally getting a glimpse of the big picture and they were ready to hit the ground running, but God hit the pause button. Instead of being given their marching orders, Jesus tells them to wait until the Holy Spirit comes. I would venture to say that not one of them thought it would end up taking ten days for the Holy Spirit to get there. Why would it take so long? I am sure that as each day came and went, they wondered that too. I think it was because God needed them, and us, to understand that things need to happen based on God's timing, not ours. In fact, this seems to be a theme in the Bible. Noah built the boat and had to wait for the rain. The walls of Jericho came down, but not until after a great deal of walking around and around.

When I was a kid, my neighbor had an apple tree in the backyard. One day my best friend and I decided to climb the tree. It was a beautiful day hanging around up there in the tree talking. I remember seeing a perfect apple hanging there. It was a bit difficult to reach and when I did it didn't want to come off the tree easily, but I was persistent. I polished that apple clean with my shirt and took a big bite. I can still remember how fast I spit it out. It tasted awful! I learned that day that no matter how good it looks, until an apple is ready to be eaten, it isn't as good as one that is truly ready. Once again, God's timing is so much better if we could learn to wait.

There were a few years in between that night at the Woman of Faith conference and when God revealed His plan for *The Twig* to me. I can tell you that the wait was hard but it was worth it. Now as I put all the pieces of my life together, I can see an obvious road leading to this moment but at the time, there was nothing obvious about it. I could never have imagined what He was preparing me for and the blessings He was going to give me.

God often uses what may seem like the pauses of our lives to grow our prayer life and our relationship with Him. In the book of Matthew there is a story of Jesus and the disciples in a boat during a storm. Have you ever wondered why Jesus slept on the boat while the storm raged on, terrifying the disciples? Why the pause to action? He waited until they came to Him for help before He did anything. He had to let them get to a place where their only hope rested in Him. If you want to see a miracle, then you have to be willing to sit in the pause. God wants us to talk to Him instead of trying to handle it ourselves. I learned this lesson from my mom. My mom hated to iron. That may not seem like a huge problem to most of us these days, but this was a time in history when everything had to be ironed, including handkerchiefs and sheets. My mother had all kinds of things that she would rather be doing than spending hours upon hours every week ironing.

I remember her telling me about the day that all changed and she fell in love with ironing. There she was, once again, in the hot basement with piles of ironing in front of her. At first, she complained to God about the task in front of her and then He opened her eyes. Every one of these items in the pile represented a blessing God had given her. A nice home, a loving, hard-working husband, and three beautiful children (Sorry, I couldn't resist adding that).

Slowly she began to thank God for each of her blessings that these things represented. Then she started to pour out her dreams and concerns to God and before she knew it, she was almost done with her ironing. From that day forward, when my mom would iron she would pray for the person who was going to use the item being ironed. Mom's attitude about ironing changed that day and she went from hating ironing to loving it. She began to look forward to those hours in the basement, the hours that were now her quiet time with her Lord. Mom began to love this time so much that she started to iron for other people and as she did, she prayed for them and their families too. God had used this moment to grow her prayer life and her relationship with Him. Once again, I love how creative God is. Who would have thought that God could use a pile of laundry to change a life?

I can now see that, like my mother, God wanted to use the pause in my life to grow my relationship with Him. To help me to learn to lean on Him, and to trust Him.

What do you

think God has been

trying to

teach you

in the

pauses of

your life?

*"Your life may not look like you imagined
but may it be what God intended."*
—DEATH ON THE NILE

Chapter 8

What if Our Journey is for a Reason?

The stepping stones of your journey won't look like mine or anyone else's. God has placed you on the stone you are on right now for a reason. It may feel like you are standing on a good sturdy stone, or it may feel a little wobbly right now. Stay strong. We each have our own path we must take to bring us to where we need to be.

So, what is the next right thing to do in your life? I like to tell my story as if it started when God revealed to me that I was to open *The Twig,* and then the next thing I knew, we were opening our doors. Technically that is true, but now I can clearly see that God had been working on my heart for years to get me to this place.

141

I was looking through some old writings of mine the other day and came across an entry that I had written almost exactly one year before God had revealed His plan for me to start *The Twig*. At the time, I had so many questions for God. Here is what I had written:

> "*Why am I like I am?*
> *I know you made me like I am but why?*
> *I want to touch others but who and how?*
> *I have gone through really hard things in my life, why?*
> *Is there a reason for it all?*
> *Lord, show me what needs to be done to show Your glory.*"

As I read those words now, I can begin to understand that God had been preparing my heart for a God-sized dream. Have you ever tried to put a puzzle together without knowing what it was supposed to look like? It's hard. None of the pieces seem to make any sense; but slowly, if you are patient, you will be able to see at least a glimpse of what can be.

> "*It makes no sense to seek your God given*
> *strength until you trust in His.*"
> —MAX LUCADO[23]

---

23 Max Lucado, *Life to the Full* (Nashville: Thomas Nelson, 2012).

Every God-given dream must start with prayer. Just a simple prayer of trust. To trust His big picture. To trust Him with your life. To trust He has perfectly designed you for the road ahead. If we can get our prayer life right, we can then change the course of history in ways we could never imagine.

As you open your heart to the will of God, you might find that He has a crazy dream for you too. Something way beyond your ability. Your God-size dream may cause you to shake in your boots, but never forget that your God is bigger than your fear.

"Don't be afraid, for I am with you. Don't be discouraged, for I am your God. I will strengthen you and help you. I will hold you up with my victorious right hand."
—Isaiah 41:10 (NLT)

God knows that we are going to face fear every day of our lives but He also wants us to understand that during every one of those days and during every one of those moments, He is there right beside us.

DON'T LEAVE GOD OUT OF YOUR STORY

If we want to have the boldness to do what the Father has for us to do, we need to start seeing ourselves the way He sees us. Jesus knew who He was. Do you know who you are in God's eyes? Take a moment and ponder Jeremiah 1:5 (NIV), "Before I formed you in the womb I knew you, before you were born I set you apart."

Let those words sink in for a moment. God knew you before you were even formed in the womb. You were His big dream. He thought about you and imagined all that you could be and then He formed you just the way He wanted you to be. Shame on us for not thinking we are not good enough! God doesn't make mistakes. Everything about you is there because that is how God wanted you.

Our job is to do what He wants us to do the best we can with what He has given us. I am reminded of days gone by when women would gather scraps of fabric to make quilts to keep their families warm. I wonder what they would think of our lives today as we try to find meaning and purpose in everything we do. These women on the prairie were just doing the best they could where they were at the time with what they had. I don't know who was the first one to look at those pieces of fabric laid out across the table and start to make them into a beautiful design, but I can imagine how excited they must have felt when it all started to come together. That is how it feels when you begin to see the pieces of your life come together perfectly. Until then, we just need to do the best we can with what we have.

I don't know about you, but my best can often feel inadequate to me. That feeling of inadequacy begins to stir up fear and causes me to question if I am where I am supposed to be. I will never forget the day that I was supposed to speak at a church about *The Twig*. The church was full of people, and I was excited to tell them how they could walk alongside us to show God's love to the foster care community. I had written every word I was going to say and yet speaking in front of large crowds was not comfortable for me in any way. I could feel my heart beating louder and louder in my chest. Before I even left my seat, my palms were sweating and every part of me wanted to run, but I didn't. The next thing I knew, I was on stage with no place to lay my notes and a microphone in my hand. I knew my topic and I was passionate about what I was about to share but I couldn't have told you my name at that moment if it wasn't written on the paper. Then suddenly it happened. All my cards hit the ground. Oh, the panic that must have shown on my face at that moment. I should have left the cards on the floor, but instead I panicked and tried to gather them up while talking at the same time. Let's just say it was terrible in every way possible. God had moved me way out of my comfort zone, and I found myself once again wondering why.

Not long after that horrific day, I began to realize that I needed to hire a full-time employee. Trusting someone else with *The Twig* was very hard for me. This was my baby that God had placed in my arms. Even though I didn't want to let go, I knew that if I wanted this ministry to outlive me, I was going to need to slowly learn to do just that. I began to pray about what that would look like and soon I knew who I needed to hire. I had arranged a job interview with a volunteer that I had and was excited at the prospect, but I had never hired anyone in my life and I had no idea what questions I was even supposed to ask her. I decided to run into the library on my way to the interview. Surely there was a book about how to interview someone. As I walked in, I quickly found a book written by a trusted author. I threw the book open, and it literally fell to a page that said, "Hire passion over skill." That sounded like good advice to me, so I closed the book and placed it back on the shelf and then ran off to the interview. It was a great interview, and I was very impressed with the passion God had already placed on her heart for what I was doing. Again, God had been preparing the journey long before I even knew the journey existed. I asked her what she felt her biggest weakness was and she replied, "Public speaking." I laughed. What might have been a red flag for me at one time no longer was. I told her that she couldn't be worse than me and proceeded to tell her my speech story. I hired her that day, and she is now one of the best public speakers I have ever heard.

God had not moved me out of my comfort zone to make me a public speaker. He did it to teach me to allow others to do the job that He had prepared them to do. God's plan was bigger than me.

God's plans are bigger than you.

Most of us have trouble seeing ourselves as God sees us. We can either think of ourselves as not good enough or we can go the other way and be so proud of who we are that we leave God at the door. Life can be such a balance of the two.

One day, when my daughter was a young girl, she sang a solo in church. It was beautiful and soon everyone started to clap and then the clapping turned into a standing ovation. In one swift moment this proud mama was taken over with fear, fear that pride would consume my daughter's life. I never wanted that desire for praise from man to overtake her desire to give God glory. Satan loves to make us proud and have us start taking credit for what is being accomplished in our lives. We must all fight this temptation daily. I now understand that this lesson on humility wasn't just for my daughter that day, it was for me.

Through *The Twig,* I have been given all kinds of opportunities to talk to all kinds of people about what I do. I admit there is still that temptation to leave God out of the story and talk about what I have been able to accomplish in such a short time. Just the other day I was getting ready to talk to a large group of potential donors and as I prepared my speech, I pondered whether I should mention God or not. Suddenly the words, "but whoever denies me before men, I also will deny before my Father who is in heaven." (Matthew 10:33, ESV) kept running through my head. Yes, this was an opportunity to bring in some really big donors alongside us but deep down I knew that God will always provide for what He wants accomplished. This again was one of those "Just do the right thing" moments. How do I leave out the One who has walked alongside me through this whole journey? I couldn't. After I spoke, multiple people commented about how they only give to Christian organizations or how they were encouraged by my story. I have come to understand that God is my story, and I must never forget that.

No matter how successful you become or how tempting it becomes, do not leave behind the One who got you where you are. It is easy to run to God when you are feeling vulnerable, but we must never forget God in our comfort. To see that He is beside us on the good days too.

I have been happily married for over forty years. One marriage secret that I have is to take time to reflect back on your love when it was young. Remember the excitement you felt. I believe that we need to do the same thing with our dreams. Take time to reflect on how God got you to where you are today and the excitement you felt as you started this journey. Never let the miracles that you have seen come to fruition become anything less than amazing in your mind.

"The great danger when God does a miracle is that we get comfortable. That's when we've got to stay humble and stay hungry. If we aren't careful, we can lose faith simply because we already have what we need. That isn't just mismanagement of a miracle, it's gross negligence."
—MARK BATTERSON, *THE CIRCLE MAKER*

I had someone tell me once that as a parent we never want to take credit for how good our kids are. Why? Because as they grow, that means we must also take the blame when they fall. Just as we must remember that our children are in God's hands, we must also remember our dreams are in His hands too. I believe this is why God often uses the unqualified to accomplish His purpose. It is so easy for us to see God in the successes when we know deep down that there is no way that we could have made all of this happen. When you know deep down that you are unqualified for the job you have been given, you know beyond a shadow of a doubt that it had to be God working through you.

My grandfather used to end all his prayers with these words, "And we will give You all the honor and praise forever and ever, amen." This is my prayer. That no matter how big or small the next task God gives me in this life, I want to give Him the glory He deserves. Because quite frankly, anything I have achieved in my life is due only to the amazing grace of God.

Anything I have achieved in my life is due only to the amazing grace of God.

If God has given you a big dream and you accomplish it, you must never forget that what He accomplished through you can also carry on without you. Let that sink in for a moment. If the dream has always been bigger than you, then God can continue it without you. As a mother I have had to learn to let my children thrive without me. The same is true with my God-given dreams.

I know that that may seem impossible in the beginning. Just like a newborn can't survive on their own, it may feel that the same is true of your dream. When we started *The Twig*, my best friend and I did everything and we did it together. We were side-by-side putting in sixty hours a week. At first it was exciting, but it quickly grew and we had nothing left to give. I began to see that if I hold onto my dream too tightly, it will never be able to grow bigger than me. It was time to start including others. As we did, I began to see the passion I felt growing in others. We now have over 150 active volunteers in addition to our employees. I have had to learn to trust others with my dream. We need to give our dreams wings so they can go places we could never take them. It's scary but it is also exciting all at the same time.

Give your dreams wings so they can go places you could never take them.

It's a great feeling, when you have been a part of something amazing. Motherhood was like that for me. When your kids are little, you are in the center of it all. It's a great feeling but then it soon becomes time for them to walk their own journey. I remember when my children got to this stage, I didn't like it. I wanted to be the center of their world forever and ever but deep down I knew that it was time to give them wings.

The truth is this is the natural progression of life. It is also the natural progression of a dream. If God has trusted you with a dream, remember to be okay with Him moving you on. This dream was never about you; it was about so much more. It's about showing people Jesus on the journey. It's about being open to God teaching you something. God made the world to evolve. A plant goes from a seed to a sapling to a plant that can reproduce. The original plant is no longer there, but the field is now full and that is a beautiful thing.

"The unprepared mind cannot see the outstretched hand of opportunity."
—ALEXANDER FLEMING[24]

My daughter got me a beautiful children's book for Mother's Day this year called *Maybe* by Kobi Yamada. I love all her books. They are not just thought-provoking, but they are beautifully illustrated. At one point in the book, it says:

"Maybe you are here to shine a light into places that have been dark for far too long? Maybe you will speak up for those who can't speak for themselves? Maybe you are here to help in ways that only you can?"

---

24 "Alexander Fleming Quote," AZ Quotes. https://www.azquotes.com/quote/1204184.

It is important that, no matter where God has brought us, we continue asking Him to show us what He wants us to see. It is often in our busyness of doing good things that we can totally miss the things that God is trying to open our eyes to.

If we can learn how to be intentional about our lives, then we will have the ability to figure out the life we want based on our core beliefs. Your core beliefs are how you see the world and your role in that world. They are what we base our lives on. The things that stand true no matter where life takes us.

Here are mine:

» I believe that we were intentionally designed by God for this time and place.
» I believe that we are to try our best to always help others see Jesus.
» I believe that with God's help we can do whatever He wants us to do.
» I believe that love should always be our guide.
» I believe that only God can give us true peace in this world.
» I believe that we are blessed to be a blessing.

Anything we have—material things, good health, and yes, even bad health—has all been placed in our lives so we can touch someone else's life. We are not designed to be an island amongst ourselves. We are designed to help those around us and to leave this world a better place because we were here. We were not designed just to consume more and more things. We are here to make a difference.

I would like to challenge you to not just think about your core beliefs, but to take the time to write them down and then become intentional about applying them to your life. Intentional living is something that we have to strive for every day of our lives if we want to feel that we have had a successful life. If you have no idea of what you believe, then I would encourage you to look back over your life. The actions of your life will speak for themselves and it will become evident to you what you value.

The first thing that people will ask when you get off a roller coaster is, "How was it?" We are quick to analyze the ride and every twist and turn along the way as we tell them all about it. Yet, for some reason when it comes to our lives, we don't look back.

Hurt, disappointment, and grief will come to us all along the way but finding the strength to get to the other side of that pain comes from being prepared ahead of time. We do that by looking back over our lives and learning who we are–accepting our weaknesses, and learning our strengths. I'm not sure which is harder - our strengths or our weaknesses. I know that sometimes I will hide behind my weaknesses but as we have already talked about, God really isn't buying the excuses. We are capable of so much more than we think. We just need to start focusing on the person God has created. He has walked you to this moment and He is not going to leave you now.

Our strengths can also be dangerous. This is when we begin to believe that we don't need God, that we can do this on our own. When God created Adam and Eve the Bible says that God walked with them in the Garden. God never intended for us to go about this life by ourselves. It's okay to lean on him. You don't have to do this alone.

SOMETHING TO PONDER . . .

What

have the

lessons

of your

life

taught

you?

"Faith is seeing beyond the horizon."
—WRITTEN IN GRANDPA'S BIBLE

Chapter 9

What if We Learned to Thrive?

ake a moment and think about what the word "thrive" looks like to you. When I think of the word thrive, it reminds me of a day I was at the gym. Oh, I was there, but I really didn't want to be. In fact, as I walked on the treadmill I was coming up with all kinds of reasons why I should just quit. You know the thoughts, "I am too busy for this." "It's not working anyway." "I just don't want to." The list in my mind kept growing as a young man in a wheelchair came in. I watched him as he struggled to go from one machine to another. In spite of it being difficult, he kept going. Where everyone else just jumped on the machines and did their workout and then moved to the next, this man struggled every time to take himself from the chair to the machine then back to the chair. Yet there he was working hard striving to do the best he could. To me this is thriving. Doing the best you can right where you are, with what you have - being the best version of you that you can be.

I used to tell my kids, *you can do anything you want to do, you just gotta want to*. The definition of the word thrive is to progress toward or realize a goal despite or because of circumstances. (Merriam-Webster) What if we could learn to thrive right where we are? What if we learned to stop making excuses and to just do it?

A few years ago, I was riding a bike from the summit to the sea on the Alaska highway - in the rain. This was not something I ever imagined myself doing and yet here I was. I remember pushing on the brakes as hard as I could and still going over thirty-five miles an hour down the mountain. No, my bike wasn't flying down this road out of control with me on it. I was actually with a group of people and two guides. But that still didn't prevent it from being a bit terrifying.

I found myself consumed with fear as I gripped the handlebar more and more tightly. I couldn't take my eyes off my front tire as I kept imagining this all ending very badly. Isn't it funny how fear can wipe away any thought of things possibly ending well?

After about five miles, I decided that if I died, I died; but in the meantime I was going to enjoy the moment. Slowly I began to take in the beauty that God had placed all around me and suddenly this crazy adventure turned into one of my most treasured memories. Life has taught me that no matter how bad a situation may seem, it will be worth it if we can learn to push through the tough and the scary.

In fact, life will often take us to places that we never imagined ourselves being. In moments like this, fear and doubt will try to derail you–but if you take your eyes off of your problems and onto God's blessings, you will find you are able to see the situation in a whole new light. We all need to remember to take a moment and reset our focus and look for the good in every situation and in everyone. We will all have twists and turns in our lives but just as the twists and turns of novels can make the story more interesting, so can the twists and turns of our lives.

EMBRACE THE JOURNEY

Alzheimer's runs on both sides of my family. I have seen generations walk this journey over the years and I will admit that it terrifies me knowing that this is a very real possibility for my future. Some have walked it better than others, but each one in their own way. When my sister started down this road with dementia, she said to me, "I used to know all kinds of things and now I don't, isn't that interesting?" My sister was just embracing the journey that God had given her. There was no fear, just a sense of wonder. I have learned that, like many things in life, you can't do anything about Alzheimer's, but you can look for the blessings it might bring. I recently found a note among my mother's things that read, "Forgetting frees me to live for tomorrow rather than being hung up on yesterday."

Ponder those words for a minute. Do you find yourself hung up on your yesterdays? Maybe your journey has brought you to a place that is hard. I get that, but it doesn't mean that you can't thrive right where you are.

Have you ever walked on a gravel road or on a rocky cliff and out of nowhere seen a beautiful flower in all its splendor? Our lives may not look like what we imagined, but if we could learn to trust Him no matter where we are, we might just find ourselves thriving in spite of the influences surrounding us and the struggles within us.

It is so easy to get caught up in our past achievements and our successes, but by doing so we can get a false sense that our work on this earth is done. Today, I googled "after a flower blooms," and this is what it said: "In its natural habitat, after the plant is done blooming, it keeps growing. During this post-blooming period, the continued leaf growth ensures photosynthesis, which in turn helps the plant store energy in the bulb for future leaf growth and flowers." We may think that this is as good as it gets, or that our glory days are over, but does God?

"It's all a process. Steps along a path. Becoming takes equal parts patience and rigor. Becoming is never giving up on the idea that there is more to be done."
—MICHELLE OBAMA[25]

There always seems to be a reason why now is not a good time. You know what I mean, the "Oh I would . . . if only . . ." Most of us are good at coming up with excuses, but what if you just did whatever it is that has been going through your head as you have been reading this book? When I was a kid, there were billboards all along the highway that said, "SEE ROCK CITY," but we never did. For one reason or another, we just kept driving. Year after year I saw those same signs, but it never seemed like a good time to stop

------

25 Michelle Obama, *Becoming* (New York: Crown, an imprint of Random House, a division of Penguin Random House LLC, 2019).

and see Rock City. It is so important that we don't get so busy in this life that we don't take the time to see what God is trying to show us along the way. There won't be billboards along life's road but if we slow down and spend time with Him, we will begin to see the possibilities all around us. Remember, God perfectly designed each of us for this world we are living in for a reason.

As I have been writing this book, I can't tell you how many times fear has swarmed me over. I am not a writer. I know that. My whole life people have made fun of my "creative" spelling and grammar. I get sayings wrong so often that my family calls them "mom-isms." It would be easy to let all those stumbling blocks stop me and let fear rule over me and once again take control of my life. But deep down I know that I have a story to tell and so I just kept writing. As months went by and my words seemed like nothing more than random sentences across the page, the temptation to quit grew stronger.

One day I looked long and hard at the delete button on the computer and almost pushed it but then I stopped. Wasn't the point of the whole book about overcoming fear? I started to laugh and started to write some more. We can't remove fear completely from our lives, but we can decide whether we are going to let it set up camp.

---

*"Faith is taking the first step even when
you can't see the whole staircase."*
—MARTIN LUTHER KING[26]

---

26 King, Martin. 1983. "New York City Speech."

If I don't say "hi" to you when I walk in a room, it is probably because I assume you would never remember me. I can't tell you why I feel this way, but I find it fascinating that God took those insecurities and opened my eyes to children that also might feel this way - children in foster care. Each of our insecurities and fears are there for a reason. God can use our fears and insecurities for His glory if we just give them to Him. Don't let Satan use them to hold you down. Our past is not there to hold us back. It is there to propel us forward. Go boldly after the person God wants you to be.

Our past is not there to hold us back. It is there to propel us forward.

JUST ONE LIFE

My Mom never talked much about her childhood, but I know she suffered great abuse as a child. Her family was very poor and her father often turned to alcohol to help him get through the Great Depression the country was going through at the time. Although she didn't talk about the abuse that she suffered, she did talk about the nice lady at the soup kitchen. This woman would smile at my mom and if my mom smiled back, the lady would then reach the spoon down deep to get the good stuff on the bottom of the pot. Mom learned, in the soup kitchen line, that if you smile at the world, it smiles back at you.

Mom taught me firsthand that we can move forward if we just set our minds to it. She used to say "If at first you don't succeed, then try, try again." Mom's smile didn't come easy. Throughout her life, things would continue to go in ways that she would never see coming; not only did she not see it coming, but it seemed she would be blindsided with tragedy everywhere she went. My mom would have to walk through all different kinds of hard days throughout her life but during those soup kitchen days, she had learned to keep smiling, no matter what. She became determined to not let her past, or even her present define her. God would define her. Are you letting your past hurts and failures define who you are or are you letting God take those hurts to mold you into the person He wants you to be?

The prayer of Saint Francis says it so perfectly:

Lord, make me an instrument of Your peace.
"Where there is hatred, let me sow love.
Where there is injury, pardon.
Where there is doubt, faith.
Where there is despair, hope.
Where there is darkness, light.
And where there is sadness, joy."

My mom wrote a paper as a young girl on how she wanted to be a missionary someday. It is the only piece of schoolwork that she ever kept. I am sure that if I had asked her, she would have probably seen that as an unfilled dream but was it really? My mom spent her life being intentional in sharing her faith. Mom prayed with strangers in Goodwill and handed random people at church money when she felt God telling her to do so. Even after she had advanced Alzheimer's, the staff of the facility would all go to her room as they came on duty for her to pray over them. Mom was always looking for ways that God might want to use her. Years after her death people would still come up to me and tell me how she touched their lives. Our lives will rarely look like what we imagine but that doesn't mean we failed.

My mother had a life motto that hung on her wall most of my life. "Only one life twill soon be past; only what's done for Christ will last." She repeatedly told this to her family and anyone that would listen. These words guided her days and now these words are etched on her gravestone so that the words that she lived by can encourage and inspire all that walk past.

God has a dream for each of our lives. They may not look like we imagined but we need to trust Him through all of life's changes. We need to trust that God is working, even if we can't see it at the time. Don't be afraid of the pause. God is still there; He just isn't ready to reveal His plan to you just yet. But maybe like that flower, in this post-bloom period, we are supposed to keep growing.

God's dreams for you can be exciting but they also might be a bit frightening. It is easy to become fearful that if we make a wrong choice we will mess up all of God's plans. Fear can cause us to become paralyzed and unable to move forward. We need to get over ourselves. God doesn't need us. He wants us. He can and will accomplish what He wants done in this world with or without us. I like it when my granddaughter makes cookies with me. Not because I can't do it without her but because I want a relationship with her. God wants to use us because He knows that it will draw us closer to Him.

Ask a teacher to describe a good student and they will probably say: "someone who is eager to learn, listens to the teacher, and takes what they have learned and applies it." It is important that each of us strive to be a good student, eagerly looking for what God might be trying to teach us in every situation and applying what we have learned to our lives. Not someday but today.

I just walked past the laundry room and there sat a load of laundry that I meant to put in the dryer yesterday. I was reminded of the saying, "You are known by your actions, not your intentions". I think all of us have things that happen every day that we intend to do and yet for some reason we don't. There might be a good reason or maybe we just haven't gotten around to it for one reason or another. My brother-in-law told me once that "our biggest obstacle in life is the front door." Isn't that the truth? So often we let the comfort of where we are, prevent us from moving forward. There always seems to be so many things that we thought we were going to do but "someday" never came.

Personally, I hate doing hard things and I find it particularly easy to put off things that I'm not sure how to do. We all like easy paths that are well-marked. Ones that we understand what might be required of us along the way. The world, and all that it involves, is open to us if we stop making excuses. If we stopped thinking about the term "What if'" in the negative form and began to see it and wonder: *What if* God wants to use me? *What if* I stepped out in faith? *What if* God has a miracle He wants me to see?

My faith journey has taught me that we never really know what tomorrow will bring, we just need to trust the One that does: God. When I started out on my nonprofit journey, I had no idea what the future would look like. God had sent me on a journey to not just grow my faith and prayer life but to also build my trust in Him. God has taught me over and over again to not run ahead of Him nor lag behind Him. I am just supposed to walk closely with Him.

"The Father doesn't give life directions in one big bundle because the goal is knowing Him not the plan."
—Louie Giglio[27]

God spent years preparing a path for me to learn from, long before He revealed His plan for me to open *The Twig*. A path that I couldn't even begin to see at the time but is so clear to me now. He had spent years gathering amazing people around me with all the right skills and talents that would be needed for this journey. While I thought He was doing nothing, in reality He was working behind the scenes making sure I was going to have everything I would need to succeed. It reminds me of when Moses explained to God all the reasons why he couldn't be a leader. Moses was explaining to God that he wasn't a good speaker, so he

---

27 Louie Giglio et al., *Passion: The Bright Light of Glory* (Nashville, TN: W Publishing Group, an imprint of Thomas Nelson, 2014).

was obviously not the right guy for the job that God was wanting to accomplish. Does this sound familiar to you? It sure does to me. I find I question God's wisdom often. It's not something I am proud of but sometimes what He is asking of me just doesn't seem to make sense. I love when Moses questioned God, and God said, "Moses, your brother Aaron is a good speaker and he is on his way." God knew Moses' weaknesses and He already had a plan in place. God knows our weaknesses too. God never needs us to know how to do everything. He just needs us to be obedient. Trust Him, He already has a plan, even if you can't see it.

Do you have an Aaron in your life? The Bible never tells us if Aaron knew why he was going to see Moses. Did God tell Aaron that Moses needed him, or did he just think he was off on a daily stroll when he happened upon Moses? It doesn't really matter; the point is Aaron had a willing heart which is good because Aaron would later become vital to the mission that Moses was about to embark on. Do you have a willing heart?

I have been blessed with many Aarons as I have journeyed through the nonprofit world, people who had skills I don't possess. Ones that I didn't even know that were needed until they showed up. Maybe you are supposed to be an Aaron in someone's life. Sometimes we get so focused on not knowing what big thing we are supposed to do when we are just supposed to walk beside the person God has put in our path. Each of us has skills and gifts that can help someone else.

With a house full of girls, it was not easy to keep their self-esteem in check as they were growing up. They were so different from each other and sometimes those differences caused jealousy to flare. I used to tell them that God had created our family to be a great team. Each one with different gifts and talents. They weren't different from each other because God made a mistake. No, God knew that we would not be nearly as effective if we all had the same gifts. We all need to stop looking at how God didn't make us and start focusing on our strengths and why God brought us together.

It is so easy for all of us to get caught up in comparing ourselves with those around us. Almost as if we think that God has put us on this earth to compete with each other. We had a missionary in our home a few weeks ago. I was in awe as I sat there listening to his story and all he has been able to do in Africa, but when he left I found myself feeling inadequate. I couldn't help but think that, compared to him, I had done absolutely nothing for God. It can be so easy for us to get caught up in comparing ourselves with those around us. The question that we need to ask though is; is it our desire to impress other people or to impress God? God doesn't measure things the same way the world does. The size of the job God gives us isn't important. What is important is our willingness to do what is asked of us.

The Bible talks about a widow that came to the temple with all she had. She found herself surrounded by others who had grand gestures that they were offering to God, but there she was with just two small coins. Did she think that what she had wasn't enough? Did she almost not even bother to come due to a sense of inadequacy? I don't know what was going through her mind as she stood there waiting her turn to place those coins in the collections box, but Jesus saw her that day. He looked past her simple gift and saw her heart. All God ever wants from us is our heart. When we give him that, God can take ordinary people without much to offer and do extraordinary things. We just need to be willing.

All God ever wants from you is your heart.

When we adopted our baby girl out of the foster care system, I thought I was up for the task. I knew beyond a shadow of a doubt that God placed this child in our family. But let me tell you the rest of the story.

We already had children who were 16, 14, and 10 years of age when we brought our baby home and that made for some challenges. We had a busy life and a busy home. With so much coming and going in and out of our house, I worried that she would never really understand who her family was. So we decided to do a family bonding trip. "This will be fun," I told myself as I loaded six suitcases, six carry-ons, a portable crib, a stroller, and a car seat onto the plane. Oh, and let's not forget the ever-present diaper bag.

I remember that first night in the hotel room. There we were - the teens sharing a bed, my ten-year-old on a roll away, and the pack-and-play stuck in the only open space in the room, and all of our luggage thrown about. It was a packed room, to put it mildly. That night I looked around as everyone was sleeping, except me and the baby. I was doing everything I could to try to get her back to sleep before she woke everyone else up, and I will admit

I had a moment of "What was I thinking? Can I really do this?" Doubt was trying to take over, but I knew this child was supposed to be a part of our family so I pushed those thoughts away and bonded with my baby.

Satan loves to use our doubt to steer us in a different direction. Hold on tight to what you know as truth. When we first started talking about the possibility of adopting a child, I talked to my dad about my fears and the "what ifs" that kept seeping into my mind. My dad was the king of worry but that day he looked at me with such compassion in his eyes and reminded me that we will never know what tomorrow will bring us but we can't let the "what ifs" rule our lives.

My dad's advice has helped me see others that walked past the "what ifs" of worry and changed the world. Think about David in the Bible. He was just a boy who thought he was given a simple task to deliver lunch to his brothers on the battlefield. To him it was probably just like any other day and yet when he got there, everything changed. As he was walking up to camp, he heard Goliath bad-mouthing his God. He looked around and was astonished that no one was doing anything about it. David knew he couldn't just stand still and let him continue. David didn't care if he had what he needed for the task before him; he just knew he had to do something. He didn't listen to the "what ifs." What if we learned to stop listening to the "what ifs" in our heads?

I saw a sign the other day that read "Live your best life." I would like for you to take a moment and imagine what your best life would look like. What if you could dream like you had no fear? What would your dreams be?

What dreams have you buried deep inside of you, afraid to share with anyone? Take a moment right now and think about the "what ifs" in your mind. If you could do anything to change the world, what would you want to change? Maybe it is to make a better cheese slicer or maybe you want to stop world hunger. A dream is a dream; don't measure your dream against someone else's. You never know where God will take it. David Green, the owner of Hobby Lobby, borrowed $600 in 1970 to sell picture frames from his home. He was twenty-nine at the time. Forty-two years later, because of his success, he has been able to give away over 500 million dollars. I am sure that Mr. Green had no idea where his dream would go. Don't limit your dreams.

When I started dreaming about *The Twig*, I thought I would just be handing out some clothes to kids that I had purchased at Goodwill. I couldn't have imagined where God was going to take it. In fact, if I had, I probably would have ran in the other direction.

Has God placed something on your heart that you have wondered why no one else is doing anything about? Maybe that is because you are the one that He is calling. You may not feel qualified for the job but time and time again we can see in the Bible where God didn't choose who the world would say was the best candidate. Look no further than who bore His son—a young, unwed girl who had nothing to offer but love and obedience. Maybe that is all that is expected of any of us: love and obedience.

When I started out on my nonprofit journey, I couldn't understand why God picked me and especially, why now? But I knew I couldn't not do it. There are some things that are not supposed to just stay in our heads, we need to share them with others.

There is another great children's book that was written by Kobi Yamada and beautifully illustrated by Mae Besom entitled *What Do You Do with an Idea?* It is about this boy who has this little "pet" that follows him around. It's not really a pet, it just looks like one. It is actually his idea. He likes his idea, but he worries about what others will think of his idea. Soon the idea begins to grow and so does his love of the idea. In the end he comes to understand that what you do with an idea is how you change the world. The book is so much better than I have portrayed it here, but it gives you an idea of why it spoke to me.

I too had an idea. I loved my idea and spending time with it, and soon realized that maybe my idea and I, together, could change the world, or at least someone's world; but to do that, I had to get it out of my head and start making it a reality. We only get one shot at this life. It is vital that we are a good steward of the life God has given us, including our dreams.

What has God

opened your eyes

to and what is

stopping you

from doing

something about it?

"*I have one life and one chance to make it count for something. My faith demands that I do whatever I can with whatever I have to try to make a difference.*"
—Jimmy Carter[28]

28 "Jimmy Carter Quotes," AZ Quotes, n.d., https://www.azquotes.com/quote/422641.

Chapter 10

What if We Started With Prayer?

hen I first got married, my husband and I lived a couple of hours from "home." Every Monday morning my mom would call me and say, "Did you go to church yesterday?" And every Monday I would scramble to come up with another reason why we hadn't. Soon we began to realize it was just easier to go to church than it was to make up another excuse for why we hadn't. The truth is finding a church can be hard. Walking into a church for the first time can often make you feel like you have just crashed someone else's family gathering, but we made ourselves do it Sunday after Sunday looking for where we were supposed to land.

One Sunday, my husband and I decided to go to this cute little church not far from our apartment. After the church service, the pastor came over to us to talk. He was a nice man and as we talked, for some reason, I decided to mention my grandfather in Iowa and how he was a pastor. As I did, the pastor looked at me with a look of astonishment and started to open up his Bible. There, on the first page of this random preacher's Bible was my grandfather's name. The pastor of this random church that we just happened to attend, near where we happened to be living, just happened to be preaching out of the Bible that my grandfather happened to give him years beforehand. You can only imagine the chill that went down my spine. Only God could have orchestrated this, but why?

It wasn't until this moment that I came to fully grasp those words in Deuteronomy 31:8 (NIV) "The Lord Himself goes before you." No matter where our journey takes us, God is one step ahead of us. We have no reason to fear our tomorrows because God is already there. The older I get, the more comfort and strength I find in that.

God cares about the details of our lives because each detail helps develop the big picture. If you have ever watched someone paint with oil paints, you can get an idea of what I am talking about. When they start, they may paint the whole canvas with a blue color, but blue is just the beginning. As the artist continues working, more and more colors are added on top of that blue and before long you have a picture of a beautiful bouquet with just a glimpse of blue in the background. Things may not always make sense to us, but in the artist's hands it will all work out.

IT'S OKAY TO NOT UNDERSTAND

When I was a young mom, I was having one of those hard days that moms of young kids can often have. The day was full of those "But why mom?" moments. I was tired and trying to provide an answer for everything, and soon I just burst into tears and yelled, "I don't know! Don't you understand that I am just a little girl trapped inside a grown-up body?"

I can still remember the shock on my daughter's face. I felt bad but that was truly how I felt. Many years have passed since that day and I'm not sure I feel much older today than I did then. There is still a part of me that will always be that frightened little girl wondering why.

It is important that we don't get discouraged and overwhelmed when we don't understand the why's in life. We may never understand this side of heaven and we need to learn to be okay with that. What if the reason behind our walk of obedience is for not for us to see? What if our obedience is for future generations? Moses never got to see the Promised Land but because of his willingness to do what God wanted him to do, many did. We may never see the big picture but that doesn't mean there isn't one. I have no idea why or when my grandfather gave this pastor the Bible, but I am sure at the time my grandfather had no idea that it would be for me to see all those years later.

We try so hard to make it all make sense but 2 Corinthians 5:7 (NIV) says, "For we live by faith, not by sight." God knows that we will always have more questions. Questions that can often paralyze us and keep us from moving forward. Since the beginning of time, God has just wanted us to trust Him with our days and move past our inquiring minds.

When my uncle was dying of brain cancer, I remember him telling me that if cancer was going to live inside of him, then this cancer was going to have to praise Jesus too. I think the same is true of our insecurities. If they won't leave, then they need to be a part of our praises.

I saw a sign once that said, "We are all broken, that's how the light gets in." It is often in our brokenness that we first begin to notice the light living deep inside of us. Our story is for a reason and it is our job to share the stories of our lives so others may not just learn what we have learned along the way but that they too may begin to look for the light shining in them. We each need to be a good steward of the story we have been given.

Be a good steward of the story you have been given

Age has taught me that this moment right now is all we have. We can't bank on our tomorrows, and we can't rest in our yesterdays. As long as we have breath in our lungs, God can and will use us. We just need to pray daily for God to give us His eyes and His heart, to not just see ourselves as He sees us, but see the world as He sees it - to understand what part He wants us to play in making the world a better place.

When I was in the middle of my darkest of days my prayers were focused on my negative feelings instead of God's assurances. That all changed that night at the Woman of Faith conference. On that night I came to understand that I didn't have to have my life all together in a neat little package for God to love me and use me. Since that day Satan is constantly trying to get me to forget all that because with that knowledge, he knows that the possibilities are endless.

In Matthew 19:26 (NIV) Jesus says, "With man this is impossible, but with God all things are possible." The Bible actually says "But God" fifteen times. God knew that we would need to be reminded over and over again that maybe we can't "But God" can.

I love this prayer from Maria Shriver in her book *I've Been Thinking . . . .*

"Dear God,
You are the God of transformation. Help me to be brave. Help me
to trust you and believe that I am here to write my life story in a
way that brings glory to you and joy to myself and others.
Amen. "

BECOMING A PRAYER WARRIOR

One day, when my daughter was a teenager she walked out of her bedroom and announced, "God told me He wants me to go to Romania!" I remember looking at her and saying, "That's nice but God didn't tell me so you aren't going." The truth is I didn't even know where Romania was on the map. There was no way I was sending my teenager there. In my mind the conversation was done. Yet weeks later, I too found myself just as excited as her as we were making plans for her first of many mission trips to Romania.

What had happened in the meantime? I wasn't talking to my daughter about Romania but the problem was, I also wasn't talking to God about it either. That didn't stop God from talking to me. The truth is I had never even asked God if she had really heard from Him. In my mind I had closed the door on Romania, but it quickly went from a country that I had never heard of to a country that I couldn't stop hearing about. Romania was suddenly everywhere I went. I went into the bakery and the people there were from Romania. Romania was on the news and in magazines in the doctor's office. I can't begin to tell you all the ways that God was talking to me about Romania. Soon my husband and I laughed and said, "Maybe we need to look into Romania." God ended up sending her there multiple times over the next few years. Romania was a part of her journey, but it was also part of mine. God was teaching me to have His eyes. To actively look for what He wants to show me. Daily we are given opportunities to trust Him but it is our job to take the step.

"The value of constant prayer is not that God would hear us but we would hear Him."
—William McGill[29]

---

29 "William J. McGil Quotes," AZ Quotes, n.d., Win and Fly LTD, 2023. https;//www.azquotes.com/quote/586093.

My grandfather was probably the strongest man of God I have ever known because he was a mighty man of prayer. I used to tell people that if my grandfather had ever met you, he was still praying for you. Every night he would fall on his knees and present his requests to God. These evening prayers would go on and on as he laid every situation at God's feet. Grandpa's prayers weren't casual prayers as if he was talking to his best friend. It was more like he was humbling himself as he approached the King of Kings. Grandpa would lay his burdens down and walk away with a peace that passes all understanding.

I have always admired my grandfather's prayer life. Grandpa always seemed to have a special relationship with God, but he didn't just wake up one day and say, "I'm going to become a great man of prayer." It was a journey that God had taken him on over the years that brought him to his knees.

As our country was in the midst of World War II, many boys from Grandpa's little church signed up to serve their country. As each of these boys left to fight, Grandma and Grandpa prayed over them, asking God to protect each and every one of them. As months turned into years and fear continued to grip the hearts of many, they continued to comfort their church body.

Then, on a day that seemed just like any other day, they got word that their son had died in a plane crash. I can't imagine the grief that must have come over them that day. Out of all the boys that went to war from their church it was only their son who didn't return–their oldest–Grandpa's namesake. At the time, they had two other boys in the thick of the war across the ocean. I can't imagine the heartache and fear they must have been experiencing.

> *"The secret is Christ in me, not me in a different set of circumstances."*
> —ELIZABETH ELLIOT[30]

I wonder if Grandma and Grandpa felt their congregation watching them to see if they truly believed what Grandpa had been preaching all these years? I don't know for sure, but I would guess that this was a time of real testing of Grandpa's faith. We all have them, times in our lives when what we have said we believe has to be acted upon. It is in times like this when others will be looking to see if our faith will stand up during the hard times. They want to see if we really believe what we have been telling others to believe. During these times we have to dig deep to figure that out too.

By the time Grandpa was in his 40s, he had suffered the loss of his mother, lived through the Great Depression, lost a son to war, and lost his first grandchild to a terrible accident, to just name a few. Many people who go through trials like this might turn away from God; but instead, my grandpa clung tighter to the One he had placed his trust in. The One who had comforted him through it all.

> *"I am not what happened to me. I am what I choose to become."*
> —CARL JUNG[31]

---

30 Elisabeth Elliot, *Keep a Quiet Heart: 100 Devotional Readings* (S.l.: Flemming H Revell, 2022).
31 "Carl Jung Quotes," AZ Quotes, n.d., Win and Fly LTD, 2023. https://www.azquotes.com/quote/446500.

In the years ahead there would be many times of loss and sorrow in Grandma and Grandpa's lives but they were learning through each struggle to focus on the One that had never changed. They became relentless in learning everything they could about God and making their relationship with Him closer.

Relentless–isn't that a great word? My grandson says that my husband is relentless, and I suppose he is. He always pushes through what needs to be done no matter what. What if we become relentless about pursuing God? Do you know the story that Luke shares in the Bible about Zacchaeus? He climbed a tree to see Jesus. As Jesus walked towards him, he called him by name and told him that he was going to his house. Can you imagine how surprised Zacchaeus was? Zacchaeus pursued Jesus and Jesus talked to him. Jesus wants a relationship with all of us, but He wants each of us to relentlessly pursue Him. This is what my grandpa did.

My grandparents had an office in their home with their desks set up across from each other. They would go up there every day and read their Bibles. During those times they were in the same room, but they rarely spoke to each other because they were each diving into what God wanted to tell them individually. I remember as a child sitting there observing all of this and wondering how many times they must have read these same stories. They loved finding new ways to apply those words they were reading to their lives. I now have one of my grandfather's Bibles. And I love to read the notes he wrote in the margins. Often, I will find a family member's name written near a verse and wonder why. What had been on Grandpa's heart at the time that he wrote that?

Grandpa taught me by example that the Bible isn't a book that sits on a shelf to look good, it is a textbook for our lives - one that needs to be studied and marked up in whatever way works best for us to learn. If you are like me and have trouble memorizing verses, that is okay. Learn the stories. God will teach you through them. Everything you learn about God today will help you learn to trust Him tomorrow. It doesn't matter how much you think you have read the Bible, there is always something more for you to learn. Why? Because our lives are constantly changing. The words that stick out to us today are not the same as the words that will stick out tomorrow. We are a work in progress. God wants to show us that we can do so much more if we would just keep our focus on Him.

BLESSED TO BLESS

God told Abraham that He would bless him so that Abraham could bless others. The older I have gotten, the more I have come to understand that God doesn't bless us to make our life easier. He blesses us so we can bless others.

Genesis 2:15 (NASB) says "Then the LORD God took the man and put him in the Garden of Eden to cultivate it and tend it."

Luke 12:48 (NRSV) says "to whom much has been given, much will be required."

Our blessings aren't entitlements, they are responsibilities. Once we start to understand that we will begin to see the world differently and our part in it.

Our blessings aren't entitlements, they are responsibilities.

Someone asked me recently if I had seen the whole picture in my mind before I opened *The Twig*. The answer is no. In fact, I still don't have a glimpse of the whole picture. God reminds me daily that He will continue to surprise me with what He can do.

Maybe you have no idea what dreams God has for your life. That's okay. Most of us don't until we do. It starts by being intentional about your time with God. As you do you will begin to understand the next step of your journey.

When I first told my husband that I wanted to open *The Twig* I didn't know the name, the place, or even how it would all work. All I knew was that I wanted to have a store with no cash register that gave clothing to children in foster care. I had no idea how we would pay rent or how we would get the merchandise. I didn't even know how many children in foster care were in our area. I just knew I was supposed to do it, so I stepped out in total faith. God continues to show me daily a little bit more of what the next step is. Sometimes I think I want to see the whole picture, but

God in His wisdom knows that I am not ready. Instead, He gives me a slice at a time.

A few years after we started *The Twig* someone offered the use of a 6,000-square-foot warehouse. I laughed. Why would we ever need something that big? A year later I reluctantly accepted the space and within a few short months, it was full. God has taught me to dream bigger than is comfortable.

Our job is not to understand but to pray hard for His guidance. Once we begin to understand the direction we are supposed to go, we need to hang on tightly because God's dreams can be so much bigger than you could ever imagine. Our job is to pray hard, to dream big, and to trust God. He will do the rest.

Our job is to:
Pray Hard,
Dream Big,
Trust God,
He will do the rest.

Have you ever prayed

for God

to give you

His eyes

and

His heart?

What did you see?

"Never forget that
God has blessed you
so you can be a blessing to others."
—DIANNE

www.ingramcontent.com/pod-product-compliance
Lightning Source LLC
Chambersburg PA
CBHW062105080426
42734CB00012B/2752